Jefferson's Country

Other Books by
Linda Firestone and Whit Morse
include:

VIRGINIA'S FAVORITE ISLANDS
Chincoteague and Assateague

FLORIDA'S ENCHANTING ISLANDS
Sanibel and Captiva

The Firestone/Morse Guide to
Jefferson's Country
Charlottesville and Albemarle County

by Whit Morse and Linda Firestone
Photography by Linda Firestone

GOOD LIFE PUBLISHERS

P.O. Box 26464   Richmond, Virginia 23261

FIRST EDITION

FIRST PRINTING—December, 1977

Library of Congress Catalog Number: 77-82201
ISBN Number: 0-917374-12-6

Cover Design by Jim Hawkins

Printed in the United States of America
by
Lewis Printing Company, Richmond, Virginia

Introduction

Jefferson's Country is full of so many interesting things to see. And, if you're like most of us, you have so little time to see them all. This guide shows you how to get the most out of your visit to Charlottesville and Albemarle. It provides a great amount of background information on the places you will want to visit. Later, when you're back home, you'll enjoy the pictures and descriptions.

This book tells you about the people and places for which Jefferson's Country is famous. It sketches the lives and accomplishments of some of them, devoting the most space to the greatest genius of them all, Thomas Jefferson, and to his creation of Monticello and the University of Virginia.

Walking tours take you through Jefferson's "academical village" at the University of Virginia and through the heart of old Charlottesville. The chapters on these tours are packed with interesting information on the things you will see. You'll read about such unusual things as the earth-shaking cannon blast that startled a sleeping city and the story of the entwined lovers' tree.

Even though Charlottesville and Albemarle offer a rich helping of history and beauty, you will eventually be looking for something a bit more substantial. The authors give you their personal appraisal of places to eat. Plus information on shops, accommodations, annual events and much, much more.

How to get there? When is it open? How much? It's all here.

In brief, this book will make your visit to Jefferson's Country more enjoyable and rewarding. And it makes a wonderful souvenir of your trip. University students and new residents also will find it informative and helpful.

Contents

Thomas Jefferson 1

Monticello 21

University of Virginia 36

Charlottesville & Albemarle County 46

Ash Lawn 52

Michie Tavern 55

Castle Hill... 59

George Rogers Clark Museum 61

Jack Jouett.. 65

Bicentennial Center 68

A Walk Around The University 69

A Walk Around Old Charlottesville.............. 81

Art Galleries and Museums...................... 101

Special Activities 104

Twenty-three Things To Do on Weekends 110

Restaurants 112

Shopping 135

Accommodations 138

Other Places to Visit in Virginia 141

Location, Hours and Fees of Major Attractions ... 146

Charlottesville Area Map 149

Emergency Numbers 150

Thomas Jefferson

THOMAS JEFFERSON was a man of such broad and far-seeing vision that his philosophy is as relevant today as it was when he wrote the Declaration of Independence, proposed a plan of public education and drafted the Virginia law guaranteeing religious freedom.

His ideas were often far ahead of his time. It was ten years before the Virginia legislature passed his proposed bill for religious freedom, and it was nearly a hundred years before his plan for public education was put into effect. He failed in his attempts to get Virginia and, later, the other original

1

states to abolish slavery, and he was only partially successful in getting slavery banned from the new territories to the west.

Throughout his writings, throughout his life, one theme appeared frequently and consistently: his passionate belief in human freedom and the rights of the individual. Freedom, he believed, is the "most sacred cause that ever man was engaged in."

And the depth of his feelings about individual rights can be judged by his declaration: "I have sworn upon the altar of God eternal hostility against every form of tyranny over the mind of man."

Jefferson was an aristocrat by birth and training but placed little value on this. He became the first great democrat and firmly believed in the ability of the people to govern themselves.

Jefferson's restless mind was so rich, so perceptive and so inventive that he had no equal. His quest for knowledge was ceaseless and ranged the whole spectrum of human achievements. Nothing was too small or too big for him, whether trying to develop improved seeds for his garden or designing a state capitol (Virginia).

Reading about his accomplishments makes one wonder if he was a dozen talented people rolled into one. He was a politician, statesman, lawyer, scientist, linguist, inventor, musician, writer, farmer, architect, geographer, philosopher and educator.

President John Kennedy, speaking at a dinner for Nobel Prize winners, described his guests as the most extraordinary collection of talent ever gathered together at the White House "with the possible exception of when Thomas Jefferson dined alone."

Early in his life Jefferson developed a love of the beautiful, rolling Albemarle countryside where he was born and where he built his mountaintop home, Monticello, an architectural gem. He was born on April 13, 1743, at Shadwell, the modest frame home his father had built on land cleared in the wilderness. The site where the home was located is just off Route 250 about four miles east of Charlottesville and about two miles from Monticello. (Only a marker on Route 250 indicates the site today.)

His father, Peter Jefferson, was one of the first three or four settlers in the county. A strong and vigorous man with a good mind, Peter Jefferson had no opportunity for a formal education but educated himself as best he could. Successful as a farmer, he also taught himself surveying and became deputy surveyor of the county. He later held several other county offices and became a member of the colony's House of Burgesses and one of the wealthiest men in the county.

Thomas Jefferson grew up on his father's farm amid the unspoiled beauty of the countryside, which was mostly wooded and much of it still wilderness. Lanky, freckle-faced, red-headed and inquisitive, always inquisitive, young Jefferson roamed the fields and woods near his home, storing up the pleasing sights and sounds and smells of the natural world around him and acquiring a love of nature that never left him.

Jane Randolph, Jefferson's mother, came from a wealthy, aristocratic family that ranked among the first families of Virginia. But Jefferson had a low opinion of an aristocracy based on family and wealth. In his *Autobiography* he wrote of the Randolphs: "They trace their pedigree far back in England and Scotland, to which let everyone ascribe the faith and merit he chooses." Jefferson sought to replace the "pseudo aristocracy" of privilege and wealth with an aristocracy of talent. He believed a man should not be measured by his family background and acquisitions but by what he accomplished on his own.

Through private tutors Jefferson was given the best education available when he was a boy. At the age of seventeen, he entered the College of William and Mary and graduated two years later. He then studied law under George Wythe, professor of law at the college and the outstanding lawyer in the colony. Wythe had a great influence on Jefferson and was "faithful and beloved Mentor in youth and my most affectionate friend through life."

Though most students of his time spent only a year or two studying law before seeking to practice, Jefferson devoted five years of intense study before he sought admission to the bar, passed, of course, and began his law practice. This concentrated effort was the way Jefferson approached everything.

3

He was a perfectionist, never satisfied with doing anything half-way.

Jefferson soon became a successful and busy young lawyer. Since his father had died some years previously, it was necessary for Jefferson to spend considerable time overseeing the family plantation at Shadwell. Yet he found time to read voraciously and to enjoy the social life of Williamsburg.

More significantly, he was now in a position to bring into reality a dream that he had nurtured in his mind since he was a boy — to build a home of classical beauty on top of the mountain he called Monticello, "the little mountain," part of the 5,000 acres of land he inherited from his father. Early in 1768 he began leveling the top of the mountain for the construction of this villa but it was not until forty years later, after many changes and revisions, that Monticello was finally completed.

His family home, Shadwell, was destroyed by fire in February, 1770, and later that year Jefferson moved into the only place at Monticello that was ready for occupancy, a small brick building at the south end of the terrace. This one-room lodge served him "for parlour, for kitchen and hall . . . for bed chamber and study too."

During that same year he met and fell in love with a beautiful, popular widow of twenty-one, Martha Wayles Skelton, who lived with her father at The Forest, his estate on the James River in Charles City County, not far from Williamsburg. Martha Skelton was slender, a little above average height, with hazel eyes and auburn hair. More widely read and better educated than most women of her time, she was also an accomplished musician. This love of music especially appealed to Jefferson, who found great pleasure in accompanying her on the violin while she played the harpsichord.

They were married on New Year's Day, 1772, at his bride's home. Later that month Jefferson and his wife set out to drive to Monticello in a light horse-drawn carriage. Winter held the land in an icy grip and the snow was nearly two feet deep on the mountain. They were forced to abandon the carriage at a nearby plantation and cover the last few miles of rough mountain road on horseback. By the time they reached the top of the mountain that night, the servants were all in bed and all the fires were out. They made their way to the one-room "Honeymoon Lodge," found a bottle of wine and happily warmed themselves with its contents and their love.

Spring comes a little late to the mountain top, where the wind blows fresh and cool, but the warm sun of April coaxes the redbuds and dogwoods into bloom until the leafless woods are brightened with sprays of pink and white blossoms. Jefferson carefully recorded each new unfolding of nature, the first peach blossom, the first dish of garden peas, the ripening of the first cherries.

This was a busy, happy period in Jefferson's life. His vast land holdings were doubled when his father-in-law died in

1773. He now had some 10,000 acres in farms and woodlands scattered over three counties. A year later, in order to handle his increased responsibilities, he gave up the practice of law. He was living the life of a gentleman farmer, an occupation he preferred above all others, and he was building his dream mansion for himself and his beautiful wife, whom he deeply loved. Laughter and music were often heard on the mountain top.

But the mutterings of growing discontent could be heard throughout the colonies. The colonies' relations with the mother country were becoming strained.

Jefferson was elected a delegate to Virginia's first revolutionary convention. On the way to the convention he became ill but forwarded to the meeting what he proposed as "instructions" to delegates to be elected to the First Continental Congress. His argument that the colonies possessed the right to govern themselves was too radical for the convention. However, his views were published in a pamphlet entitled "A Summary View of the Rights of British America," which was widely read with great interest. Jefferson became known as one of the leading voices for independence.

Jefferson's reputation as a writer had preceded him when he arrived as a delegate to the Second Continental Congress, meeting in Philadelphia. The way John Adams put it, Jefferson's writings were "remarkable for the peculiar felicity of expression." And it was in recognition of his way with words that Jefferson was chosen to write the Declaration of Independence. The masterpiece he created inspired not only the people of his own land but those of other countries as well. It was courageous and revolutionary to proclaim in those days of kings and queens that "We hold these Truths to be self-evident, that all Men are created equal, that they are endowed by their Creator with certain unalienable Rights, that among these are Life, Liberty, and the Pursuit of Happiness."

That fall Jefferson returned to Virginia and carried on his fight in the state legislature to bring about a government of and for the people. He sought to erase "the ancient or feudal aristocracy" and to lay the foundation for a "government truly republican." Against heated opposition he pushed through a bill abolishing "entail," a device the aristocracy used to limit inheritance of property to certain heirs so that it could not be transferred to anyone else. The bill also abolished the practice of primogeniture, whereby the first-born son inherited practically everything and the other children got little.

But even more important was his bill for religious freedom, separating church and state and assuring every person the right to worship—or not worship—as he pleased. This bill aroused savage opposition and it took ten years of dogged effort by Jefferson's friends before it was finally passed. By that time Jefferson was serving on an assignment in France.

Jefferson, believing strongly in the freedom of man, was deeply troubled over slavery. He had included in his original draft of the Declaration of Independence a denunciation of slavery and the slave trade but this was all deleted by the Continental Congress. Now he proposed to free all slaves born after a certain date, but the Virginia legislature, dominated by

planters, would have no part of that. Years later, in 1784, when he was serving in Congress, Jefferson tried to get a bill passed to bar slavery from the West. This was defeated at the time but three years afterwards Congress did incorporate the provision into the Northwest Ordinance of 1787. Jefferson predicted that "nothing is more certainly written in the book of fate than that these people are to be free."

Jefferson believed that education was essential to the survival of a democratic form of government. "If a nation expects to be ignorant and free in a state of civilization," he warned, "it expects what never was and never will be."

He tried hard to get his state to provide an opportunity for everyone to get an education. But once more he was far ahead of his time and his plan for a complete educational system—elementary school through university—failed to get sufficient support.

A leader of his party in the legislature for over two years, Jefferson was elected governor of Virginia on June 1, 1779, succeeding Patrick Henry. His election came at a time when the British, failing to destroy General George Washington's army in the north, decided to attack from the south. Jefferson sent all assistance he could but there was not much available to send, either supplies or men.

It was a gloomy time. Virginia was in the midst of a depression, a blight destroyed much of the crops and the British were threatening the exposed borders. North Carolina was raided. South Carolina was under attack.

In January, 1781, a British force under command of the traitor, General Benedict Arnold, marched into Richmond, disrupting the government and destroying supplies. Jefferson mustered what militia he could but not nearly enough to stop the British.

Again in May the British threatened Richmond and the legislature moved to Charlottesville. Colonel Banastre Tarleton was dispatched with 250 British dragoons to capture Governor Jefferson and the members of the legislature in Charlottesville. Jack Jouett, a captain in the militia, saw the redcoats while they were still forty miles away from Charlottesville and rode all night across the countryside to warn Jefferson and the legislators in time for most of them to escape.

Lord Cornwallis meanwhile proceeded to Point of Fork, where the Rivanna flows into the James River, and made his headquarters at Jefferson's farm at Elkhill. His troops destroyed all the crops, burned the barns, used the cattle, sheep and hogs for food, killed or carried off all the horses and left the plantation "an absolute waste."

Jefferson's term as governor ended early in June and he returned to Monticello to devote his time to reading and writing and overseeing his farms. During this time he did most of the writing on his first and only complete book, *Notes on the State of Virginia,* crammed with information on Virginia and interwoven with his own opinions and philosophy. This was later published in Paris.

Jefferson was determined not to be drawn back into politics. But an event occurred that shook the foundations of his life and changed its course. His wife, who had been in failing health for months, died on September 6, 1782. His happy mountain home became a somber place of grief and despair. Hour after hour he rode along the mountain trails and through the woods, desperately and futilely trying to escape from the aching grief within him. His daughter later recalled that her father was "incessantly on horseback, rambling about the mountain." Jefferson felt his wife's death so deeply he said it "wiped out all my plans."

He was in a state of mind for a change, an escape from the place so filled with haunting memories of happy days with his wife. So he welcomed appointment to Congress and took his seat in December, 1783. As was characteristic with him, he plunged wholeheartedly into his work. Though he served less than a year, he accomplished much. He served on all the important committees and wrote most of the significant papers. One of his most valuable contributions was the proposal of a decimal system of coinage, based on the dollar, which we use today.

In May of 1784, Jefferson was appointed to a three-man commission to negotiate commercial treaties with European countries and a year later he succeeded Benjamin Franklin as Minister to France. Jefferson found Europe an exciting storehouse of art and science. He toured Southern France, Italy, England and the Rhineland, soaking up a vast amount of information on a great variety of subjects, architecture, labor-saving inventions, agriculture, wines and food. He liked French cooking so well he later introduced it into the White House and Monticello.

While in Paris, Jefferson received a request from the Virginia legislature to design a new capitol building in Richmond. His design was modeled after one of his favorite structures, the Maison Carrée at Nimes, an ancient Roman temple, which he considered "the most perfect model of ancient architecture remaining on earth." Though wings have been added to the original structure, the Virginia Capitol still retains much of the simple, classical beauty of Jefferson's design.

While Jefferson was in France, the Constitution of the United States was drawn up and General Washington was elected the first President. Washington called Jefferson home and appointed him the first Secretary of State, a position for which he was uniquely qualified. But Jefferson soon found himself in a very trying situation. Believing fervently in a democratic form of government, responsible to and controlled by the people, he clashed head-on with Alexander Hamilton, who had a low opinion of the average citizen and favored the "rich and well-born." Hamilton, to the distaste, anger and horror of Jefferson, sought to establish the English-type institutions of monarchy and aristocracy and to bring the government under the control of financial interests. Hamilton was contemptuous of democracy and its most brilliant proponent, Thomas Jefferson.

Jefferson, feeling obligated by his passionate belief in freedom to defend it against the threat of Hamilton and his self-interest groups, nevertheless detested such controversy. Unhappy, disturbed, his health suffering from the strain of unrelenting political conflict, Jefferson stayed on reluctantly as a cabinet member, persuaded to remain by President Washington. At last, in January, 1794, he left behind him the bitter, often mucky, political scene in Philadelphia and headed towards his beloved home, Monticello. He was bone-weary, the taste of politics was sour in his mouth, and he longed for that serene and peaceful mountain top where the only storms were those of nature.

After "five and twenty years of constant occupation in public affairs and total abandonment" of his own, Jefferson desired only "rest and oblivion." He returned to farming "with an ardour which I scarcely knew in my youth." And there was much to be done. He owned over 10,000 acres of land on thirteen farms but they had suffered from neglect in his absence and he was in debt. He was eager to try out improved farming practices he had observed abroad and to make some improvements of his own. Among these improvements was his invention of a moldboard plow, designed for the heavy red clay soil of his native Albemarle. This invention won him a gold medal from the Agricultural Society of Paris.

Jefferson's hand did not guide a plow or lift a hoe. Yet he felt close to the soil and loved its cultivation. "No occupation," he once wrote, "is so delightful to one as the culture of the earth, and no culture comparable to that of the garden."

At this time, Jefferson was able to resume his labor of love, building Monticello, changing and improving his original plan to incorporate the ideas he had gleaned from his European travels.

Happy though he was, he was not long left to enjoy a busy, peaceful rural life. His political party pressed him into service in 1796 as its presidential candidate against John Adams. It was a close contest. Adams, with 71 electoral votes, became President, and Jefferson, with 68 votes, became Vice-President, as was the practice in those days.

Jefferson thought the vice-presidency would be "honorable and easy." Events proved him wrong. England and France were at war and France's attacks on American shipping and contemptuous attitude towards America drove the country to the brink of war. Adam's party, the Federalists, seized upon this as an opportunity to stamp out Jefferson's Republicans (forerunners of today's Democrats). The Federalist Congress passed the Alien and Sedition Acts. The Alien Law gave the President the right to deport anyone he judged dangerous to peace and liberty, and the Sedition Law virtually canceled the Bill of Rights, providing large fines and prison sentences to anyone who conspired to oppose government measures. These were aimed at silencing any opposition and destroying

Jefferson's Republican party under the smokescreen of the threat of war.

To combat the vicious attacks by the Federalists, Jefferson secretly wrote the Kentucky Resolutions passed by the Kentucky legislature, declaring the Alien and Sedition Acts unconstitutional. Virginia passed similar resolutions.

In the presidential election of 1800, Jefferson ran against Adams. The Federalists savagely attacked Jefferson, calling him just about every evil name imaginable. One venemous political writer predicted "murder, robbery, rape, adultery and incest will be openly taught and practiced" if Jefferson were elected. These absurd, false and vicious attempts to smear Jefferson hurt him inwardly. He must have wanted to crush some of the most unscrupulous of his tormentors under his heel but he remained outwardly calm. And he won the election, defeating Adams by 73 electoral votes to 65. But Jefferson's running mate Aaron Burr also got 73. This threw the election into the House of Representatives, where the Federalists did their best to keep Jefferson from the position he was meant to have. Finally, after thirty-six ballots, Jefferson was elected the third President of the United States.

Jefferson's election brought about a change in the government. The Federalists, more a party of the aristocratic and the wealthy, were replaced by the Republicans (today's Democrats), who were more in tune with the people and less concerned about formality and ceremony. Jefferson sought to limit the power of the federal government and to leave the people and the states as free as possible to manage their own affairs.

The most outstanding accomplishment of Jefferson's first term as President was his purchase of the Louisiana Territory. For fifteen million dollars, a price that seemed large then but small now, Jefferson added 800,000 square miles, almost doubling the size of the United States. As gigantic a step as that was, Jefferson had a vision of an even bigger nation, extending all the way to the Pacific Ocean. He got Congressional approval for an expedition to explore the vast northwest and picked Captain Meriwether Lewis of Albemarle County, his private secretary, to head the expedition. Lewis chose William Clark to share the responsibilities of the expedition. They started from St. Louis and traveled up the Missouri River into the unknown wilderness, finally reaching the mouth of the Columbia River where it flows into the Pacific Ocean. They made it back to St. Louis two years and four months after the start of this remarkable expedition.

Jefferson's purchase of the Louisiana Territory had caused his popularity to soar. His election to a second term was assured. In his second inaugural address, he reminded his listeners that his administration had pursued a course of

peace and had cultivated "the friendship of all nations." At home, he pointed out, the elimination "of unnecessary offices, of useless establishments and expenses" had enabled his administration to "discontinue our internal taxes."

This was a time of peace and good feeling. But it was not to last for long. Europe was locked in the Napoleonic War. Both France and England ignored America's neutrality. Britain attacked American shipping at will and, most infuriating of all, forced thousands of American seaman to serve on British ships. Jefferson, who said "peace is my passion," searched desperately for a way to stay out of the war. His attempted solution was an embargo banning American shipping from the oceans. This effort at "peaceful coercion" was a noble attempt and did keep the United States out of the war for the time being but it was ineffective. The embargo worked greater hardship on this country than on Britain and France and, since the United States did not have the means to enforce it, smuggling became widespread. Jefferson came under heavy criticism. Against his wishes, near the end of his term, Congress voted to repeal the embargo.

Jefferson was more eager than ever to return to Monticello.

As he expressed it in a letter, "never did a prisoner, released from his chains, feel such relief as I shall on shaking off the shackles of power."

Ah, how good it was to be back at Monticello! Now in his sixty-sixth year, Jefferson was in excellent health, keen of mind and vigorous. Although he had retired from the demands and vexations of the Presidency, he led an active life, more active and productive than many men much younger. He was up early and devoted his mornings to correspondence. Then "from breakfast to dinner [mid-afternoon], I am in my shops, my garden, or on horseback among my farms; from dinner to dark, I give to society and recreation with my neighbors and friends; and from candlelight to early bedtime, I read."

Jefferson's greatest accomplishment in his later years was the founding of the University of Virginia. Long ago, when a member of the Virginia legislature, he had envisioned a broad system of public education, with elementary schools at the bottom and the university at the top. The other members of the legislature lacked his vision and his proposal failed. But

Jefferson never gave up. He believed a democracy could not continue to exist without the education of its people. Once again, in 1814, he renewed his efforts to get the state legislature to adopt a plan of public education. This time he was partially successful. The legislature finally approved a state university and, in 1818, appropriated a scant $15,000 to get the university started. Jefferson had already raised by private subscription enough money to buy the land for the university and to start construction of the first buildings.

Jefferson was in every sense the "father" of the University of Virginia. He conceived the idea, labored to get it through the legislature and to raise the money, designed the buildings, supervised construction and selected the faculty.

The university opened for classes in the winter of 1825, about a year before Jefferson's death.

While he spent much time creating the University of Virginia during his last years, Jefferson was busy with many other projects, supervising his farms, experimenting with improved methods of agriculture and carrying on voluminous correspondence with friends and others asking his advice. From his stately home he could look out upon the immense panorama of valleys and mountains, stretching westward to the massive, hazy wall of the Blue Ridge, a serene and peaceful scene of majestic beauty.

18

But Jefferson's mind was not at peace. The trend of national politics was disturbing to him. Instead of the new states being free, they were divided by the Missouri Compromise into free and slave. And the nation was drifting towards a stronger federal government, weakening the powers of the states.

Visitors came to Monticello in increasing numbers to see and talk with the world-famous Jefferson, the "sage of Monticello." Feeding the constant flow of guests put a heavy drain on his dwindling resources. His farms had suffered from his long absences in the service of his country, and the years of war and the embargo had been damaging. Jefferson tried desperately to pay off his debts. He sold his cherished library to the United States in 1815 to replace the books lost when the Congressional Library was destroyed by the British the previous year. He received only $23,950 for some 6,000 volumes, less than half the original cost of the books. When the panic of 1819 struck, Jefferson was almost forced into bankruptcy. He had endorsed a $20,000 bank note for a friend who went bankrupt, leaving Jefferson to pay off the loan. Jefferson's finances reached such a point in 1826 that he felt he would have to sell his property. When Jefferson's miserable financial condition became known, mass meetings were held and some money was raised and forwarded to him. While it was not nearly enough to pay off his debts, Jefferson accepted the money as "a pure and unsolicited offering of love," justifying his belief in the goodness of the people, for whom he had given so much of his life.

All through the spring of that year, even as new life spread a thickening cover of fresh green over the mountain, Jefferson's health was declining rapidly. He was eighty-three years old and his body was worn out, though his mind remained bright and sharp and in full command of the amazing store of knowledge acquired through a lifetime of study. June, gentlest month of the year in old Virginia, brought its long days of warm sunshine and deep blue skies, but Jefferson's strength was fast slipping away. He was too feeble to accept an invitation to the celebration of the fiftieth anniversary of the Declaration of Independence in Washington. On June 24th, in the last letter he wrote, Jefferson expressed his disappointment over not being able to attend the festivities and hailed the increasing awareness that "the mass of mankind has not been born with saddles on their backs, nor a favored few booted and spurred, ready to ride them legitimately by the grace of God."

Jefferson was near death on July 2 and called his family together and bid them farewell. Fighting stubbornly with all the strength he had left, he managed to hang on until the Fourth. He died ten minutes to one o'clock on July 4, 1826, fifty years to the day from the signing of the Declaration of Independence he had written. By an odd coincidence, John Adams, his old friend and one of the signers of the Declaration, died that same day in Quincy, Massachusetts.

Jefferson was buried in the family graveyard at Monticello under a big oak where he had played as a boy. He left instructions for a plain grave marker cut from coarse stone and consisting of an obelisk six feet high, mounted on a three-foot cube. He asked that the faces of the obelisk bear only the following inscription:

"Here was buried
Thomas Jefferson
Author of the Declaration of American Independence
Of the Statute of Virginia for religious freedom
And Father of the University of Virginia."

Monticello

So much of Thomas Jefferson went into planning and building his beloved home, "Monticello," that you can probably get to know him better from a visit there than in any other way.

His prodigious talents combined to create a unique masterpiece of classic beauty and graciousness. And everywhere you look in the home, you see Jeffersonian innovations that made life more comfortable, enjoyable and efficient.

For over forty years—off and on—Jefferson was building, tearing down, changing, redesigning and adding to the main building and its dependencies. He started leveling off the top of the mountain in 1768 and by 1809 he had his home mostly "completed," though it was never really finished, for Jefferson was always planning some new arrangement, adding some new touch or installing some new device contrived by his inventive mind. "Architecture is my delight," he is supposed to have said, "and putting up and pulling down one of my favorite amusements."

Monticello, which means "little mountain" in Italian, was a lofty home for a lofty mind. Other planters built their homes on low ground along the rivers and inlets, where access by water was easy and crude dirt roads not too difficult to build. But Jefferson boldly placed his home on a mountain top, thinking the soul-lifting view worth all the effort of laboriously hacking roads out of the mountain side. From the lawns at Monticello, some 850 feet above sea level, you can look westward across the beautiful rolling countryside to the Blue Ridge Mountains, a bluish, irregular wall stretching along the distant horizon.

"With what majesty do we there ride above the storms!" Jefferson wrote joyfully of his home. "How sublime to look down into the workhouse of nature, to see her clouds, hail, snow, rain, thunder, all fabricated at our feet!"

Jefferson brought his bride to the mountain one cold, snowy night in January, 1772, several weeks after they were married at her father's plantation not far from Williamsburg. The happy couple lived in the one-room "Honeymoon Lodge" at the end of the south terrace until the main house was finished enough for them to move in two years later.

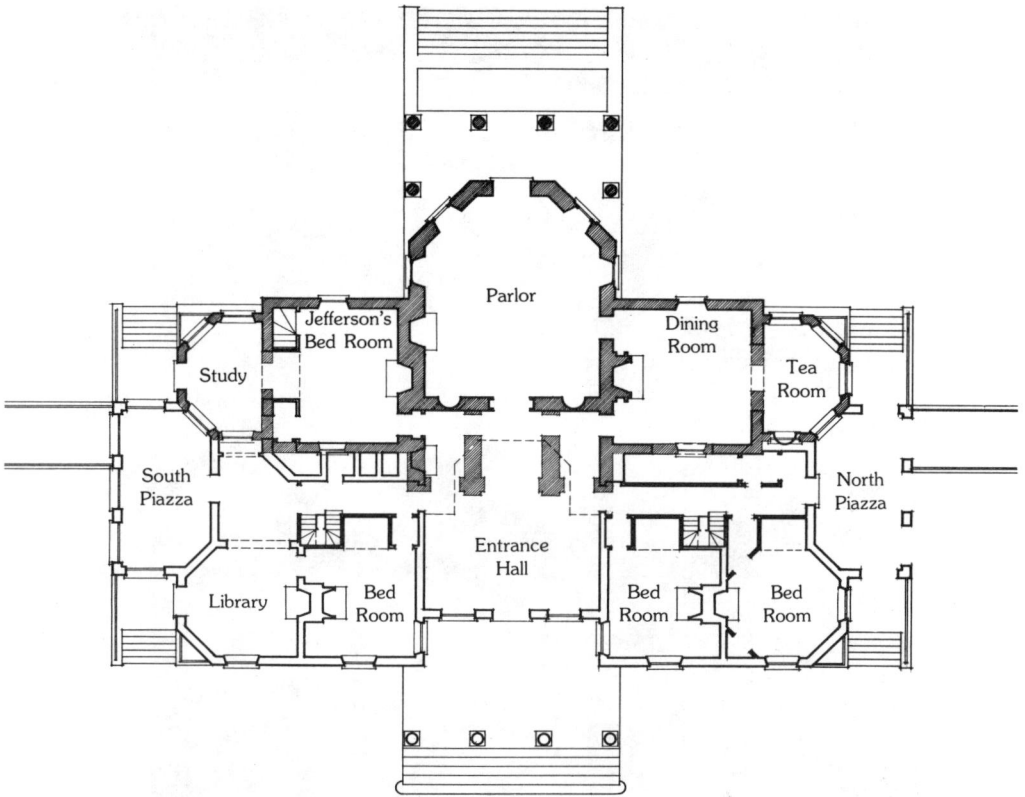

First floor of Monticello as it is today. Shaded portion shows building
before Jefferson began remodelling it after his return from Paris.

The main house at that time was less than half the size it is
today and quite different in appearance. The entrance hall
and the east portico, where you enter on your tour, did not
exist, nor did the other rooms on the east side. Instead, there
was a one-story portico, and directly above that, a second-
floor portico, though it is not known whether this upper portico was ever completed.

On the west front of the building, the big white dome, today's most remembered feature, had not yet been conceived in
Jefferson's mind. He got the idea for the dome and other addi-
tions and refinements from buildings in Europe while he was
serving as Minister to France. When he returned to this country, he began remodeling Monticello on a grand scale, erecting

the dome over the center section and putting up the west
portico, doubling the size of the house by adding rooms on the
east, building the one-story east portico and adding loggias,
"piazzas" he called them, at the north and south ends of the

building. He raised the ceilings of the main rooms on the first floor to give a spacious feeling more in keeping with the new houses of the well-to-do in Paris. Also in keeping with the Parisian fashion in architecture of the period, he built the new second-floor bedrooms with lower ceilings than the main rooms on the first floor and with small, low windows above the first floor windows, creating the illusion of a one-story building even though the house is three stories high. Looking at the house from the outside, one would hardly imagine it contains thirty-five rooms, twelve of them in the basement.

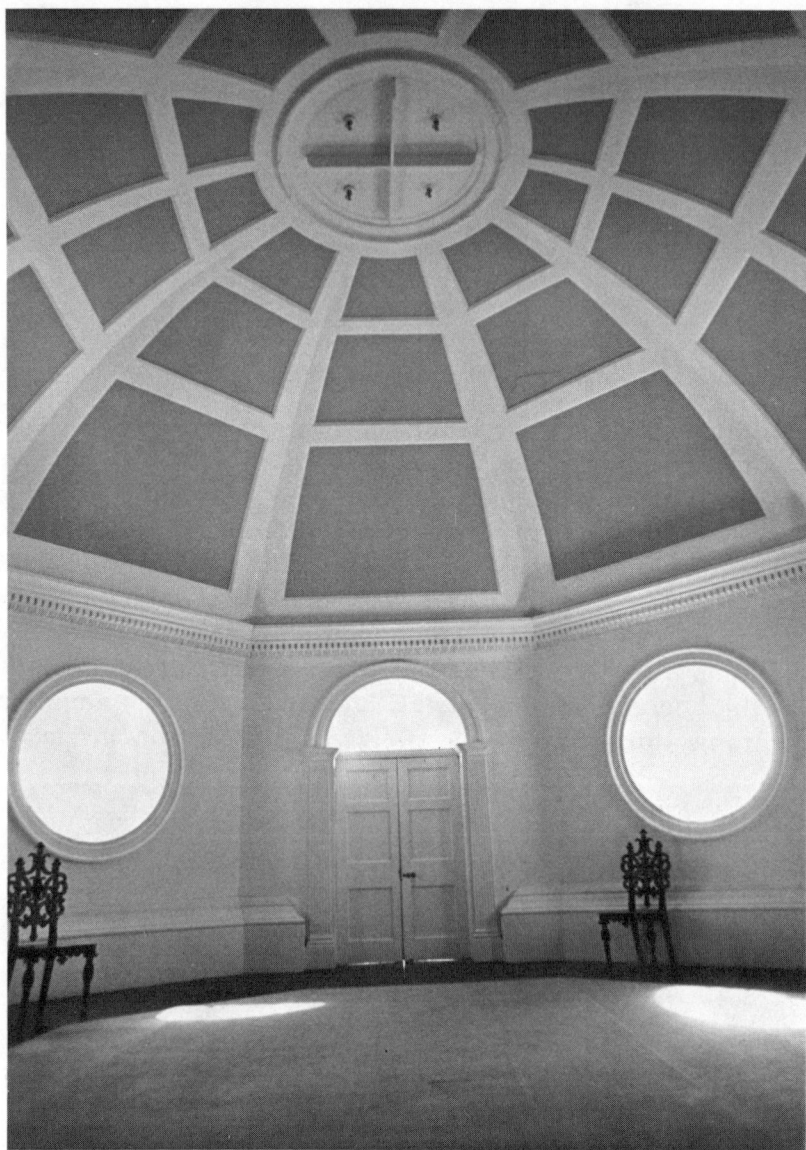

The most dramatic room in the whole house, the "Dome" or "Sky" Room, is located on the third floor. This grand room, with its ceiling lifting up to a towering apex, is octagonal in shape and has round windows, each with a dozen panes of glass set in a circular pattern. There are three third floor

bedrooms, with skylights for windows. These bedrooms are not visible from the outside.

Jefferson made other changes inside that reflected the ideas he had gathered abroad. He tore out the great stairway in the east hall and tucked away two space-saving stairways in a cross passageway. These stairs, with treads only twenty-four inches wide, zig-zag upward in a very small space.

(Unfortunately, because of the narrow stairways, the second and third floors are not open to visitors.)

On the first and second floors, he added the luxury of inside privies, a rare convenience and comfort in the United States in those days. The three privies were constructed so that shafts in the walls led straight down to an air tunnel, where there were receptacles on carts which could be rolled along the tunnel.

Another European introduction was alcove beds. All but one of the beds in the house are set in alcoves.

Jefferson's bedroom suite is located in the southwest section of the house. It consists of two rooms, a study and bedroom, with the bed alcove in between the two rooms and open on both sides, so that Jefferson could get out of bed in either room. Furniture in the bedroom suite is original, as is most of the furniture in the house. You can see his revolving chair, one of the first in this country, writing table with swivel top, and a chaise lounge, so that he could sit with his feet up while writing. A bust of John Adams, a friend he cherished, sets in a window, next to Jefferson's portable telescope, through which he could view the town of Charlottesville and see the University of Virginia taking shape. A portrait of Jefferson, painted from life when he was seventy-three, hangs over the fireplace. The alcove bed, like the others, is six feet, three inches long, just barely long enough for Jefferson, who was six feet, two and a half inches tall. While the bed might seem a little short, with only half an inch to spare, Jefferson probably followed the custom of many people in those days and propped himself up with pillows so that he was not fully reclining. Jefferson slept in this bed whenever he was at Monticello and died in it July 4, 1826.

The house has many other features inside that set it apart from other houses in his day and demonstrate the inventiveness of Jefferson. It was characteristic of him that everything he touched he sought to improve. He invented a chain and sprocket device to operate the double doors between the entrance hall and the parlor—open or close one door and the other door opens or closes simultaneously. One of the most fascinating of his "conveniences" is the big, seven-day calendar clock above the door in the entrance hall. Jefferson designed this clock to be operated by round weights like cannon balls. Eight of the weights on the north wall govern the striking of the hour by a copper gong on the roof. As the gong sounds, the balls move down the wall. On the other wall, six weights move slowly down past the names of the days, with the top ball indicating the day of the week and, approximately, the hour. Jefferson ran out of space when he designed the clock and had to cut a hole in the floor so that the weights could disappear into the basement at noon Friday and remain there until the clock is wound on Sunday (Saturday and Sunday are marked on the basement wall). The clock is wound with a twenty-two inch ratchet "key." To reach the clock, Jefferson had an ingenious ladder that could be folded into a pole and placed in a corner.

Most of the materials used in building Monticello, except for such items as window glass, locks, and sheet copper and iron for roofing, were produced on the plantation. Stone for the foundations was dug from the mountain. The bricks were molded from the red clay soil and fired in a kiln located on the place. Huge trees cut from the virgin forest were shaped into framing, floors, trim and decorative pieces. The nails were made in Jefferson's "nailery."

Floors in the house are heart pine, except for the parquet floor in the parlor. This floor, another "first" in America, is made of cherry and beechwood. The parlor was used for entertaining and his wife Martha's piano was kept there. Jefferson often accompanied her on his violin, both of them finding great joy in music.

Jefferson combined his love of architecture and his love of nature in fitting his majestic home into the mountain top in such an unobtrusive way that it seems an organic part of the landscape. As was so often the case, he was far ahead of his time, foreshadowing modern architects who consider the setting an integral part of the structure they design.

Jefferson was determined not to have the glorious sweep of the mountain top spoiled by an ugly clutter of "dependencies" found on other plantations—smoke houses, weaving houses, kitchens, store rooms, stables, ice houses, laundries and other miscellaneous structures necessary to the operation of the farms. He must have spent a lot of time going over his books on architecture and thinking about ways of making these dependencies less conspicuous. And he came up with a unique solution. He would link the dependencies together in long, L-shaped wings and sink them into the brow of the mountain in terraces at the north and south edges of the west lawn.

That's the way you see them today. At the end of each terrace is a one-room lodge, "pavilion," which opens onto a walkway on top of the terrace leading to the main house. The southern terrace ends in the "Honeymoon Lodge" and the northern terrace ends in a lodge known as the study of Colonel Thomas Mann Randolph, Jefferson's son-in-law.

Colonel Randolph's Study

Below the southern terrace there is a colonnade, and opening off this corridor are the smoke house, dairy, servants' quarters and kitchen, which is located at the bend of the "L" next to an all weather passageway under the house. The well that served the house is located in front of the colonnade. This well, sixty-eight feet deep, sometimes ran dry when there was not enough rain, and water was carried from springs on the side of the mountain. Four cisterns at the corners of the terraces collected rainwater.

Opening off the arcade on the northern terrace are stables, carriage house, ice house and laundry.

The terraces are connected by a passageway under the house. Conveniently located on this passageway are the wine room, ware room, beer cellar, "cyder" room and rum cellar. Also on this passageway are rooms converted into a museum, with many personal mementos of Jefferson, including his gold tooth-pick, calling cards, a razor set holding a blade for each day of the week, and the paint box and drawing instruments he used to make architectural drawings.

Jefferson landscaped the broad lawns of Monticello with gravelled walkways, flower beds, shrubs and trees, much the way you see them today. The fish pond on the lawn near the end of the south terrace was kept stocked with fish caught in nearby streams and carried there to await their trip to the table, a novel way to be assured of truly fresh fish.

An extensive system of roadways gave access to the orchards, gardens and farmland, which included not only the land at Monticello but adjacent farms, totalling almost 5,000 acres. Jefferson laid out a series of roads—he called them "roundabouts"—circling the mountain at four different levels and connected by other roads built at an angle in order to make the incline less steep and avoid erosion. Each of these roads had to be hacked out of a virgin mountainside covered with towering trees.

A pleasant walkway leads past the orchard and gardens (now devoted largely to flowers) down the slope of the mountainside to the graveyard where Jefferson is buried.

"All my wishes end, where I hope my days will end, at Monticello."

Thomas Jefferson Memorial Foundation

The Thomas Jefferson Memorial Foundation bought Monticello in 1923 and since that time has painstakingly restored the house and Jefferson's furnishings until you can now see it much the way it was when Jefferson lived there. The Foundation is a nonprofit organization and uses the money it receives to continue restoration and preservation of the home and the grounds.

University of Virginia

THOMAS JEFFERSON regarded his creation of the University of Virginia as one of his greatest accomplishments. Along with his authorship of the Declaration of Independence and the Virginia Statute for Religious Freedom, Jefferson ranked the University as one of the three achievements he wished to be remembered for.

Jefferson took a possessive pride in the university. And deservedly so. No other man in history can claim to be so completely the "father" of such an institution. He conceived the idea, wrote the charter and piloted it through the state legislature, raised the money through private subscription and through the legislature, drew up the plans (designing every building, column, window and door—thousands of drawings in all), supervised the construction (even training workmen where necessary), laid out the plan for the gardens, walls and walkways, served as the first rector, and selected the faculty and courses of study. Out of his genius and tremendous effort emerged a university that was "the most eminent in the United States."

His design for the university is best described in his own words: "The plan of the building is not to erect one single magnificent building to contain everybody and everything, but to make of it an academical village in which every professor should have his separate house, containing his lecturing room with two, three or four rooms for his own accommodation according as he may have a family or no family, with kitchen, garden, etc.; distinct dormitories for the students, not more than two in a room; and separate boarding houses for dieting them by private housekeepers."

Jefferson's "academical village" is recognized as one of the most beautiful groups of buildings in the United States. Its creation was the crowning intellectual and architectural achievement of Jefferson's brilliant life, and it is even more remarkable when you consider it was begun when he was seventy-five years old.

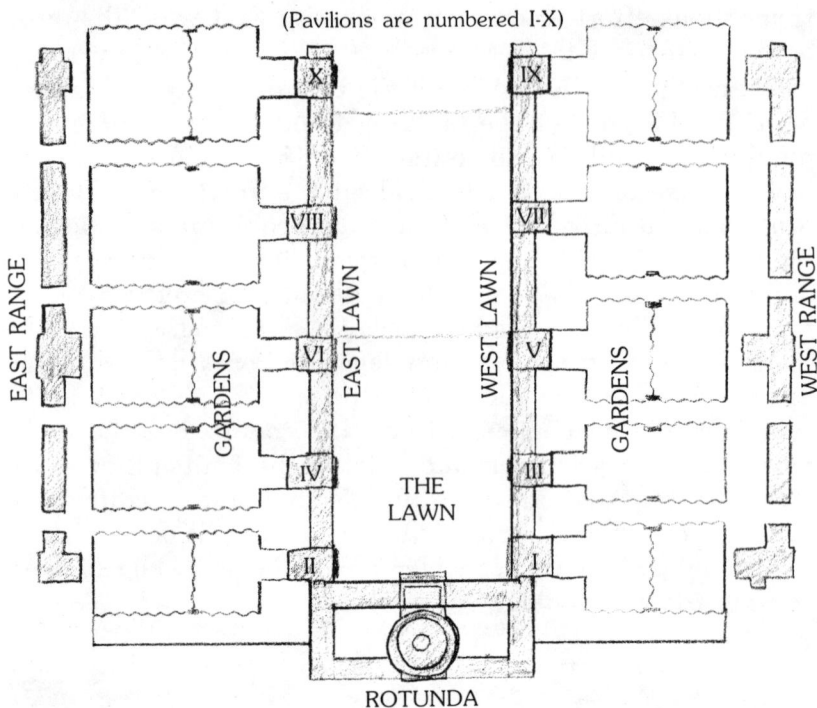

Thomas Jefferson's "Academical Village"

Focal point and dominant feature of Jefferson's "academical village" is the stately Rotunda, a modified, half-size replica of the Pantheon in Rome. The Rotunda stands at one end of a rectangle with sides formed by professors' houses (pavilions) and rows of students' rooms, with a colonnaded passageway along the front. An immense lawn some 600 feet long and 200 feet wide, dotted with trees, stretches from the south portico of the Rotunda to the end of the "village." The south end of the Lawn was originally left open but it was closed in 1899 with the erection of Cabell Hall. Before that time the south end of the Lawn had only a low wall to keep out stray cows and pigs.

38

Jefferson prepared a different design for each of the pavilions housing the professors so that they would be "models of taste and good architecture, and of a variety of appearance, no two alike, so as to serve as specimens for the Architectural lecturer." There are ten pavilions, five on each side of the Lawn. Except for one occupied by the Colonnade Club and another serving as the office of the president of the university, these pavilions are still being used as faculty residences.

Back of each pavilion is a big garden, originally used by the professors to grow vegetables and to keep pigs and cows. They ceased to be used for that purpose long ago and the gardens were planted and the walls restored by the Garden Club of Virginia. Many visitors are intrigued by the serpentine walls. These unusual walls are both beautiful and functional, with their curving design making it possible to build a strong, enduring wall only one brick thick.

Beyond the gardens are rows of student rooms, called East Range and West Range, running parallel to the Lawn on both sides. The Ranges face away from the Lawn and have colonnaded passageways along the front. Three "hotels" are equally spaced within each Range. The hotels were originally used as student dining rooms but are now meeting rooms and offices.

Rooms on the Ranges are now used by graduate students only and they are assigned by lottery. The rooms on the Lawn are assigned to outstanding seniors. Many well-known people have occupied rooms on the Lawn and the Ranges. Edgar Allen Poe roomed at 13 West Range from February to December, 1826, and this room, furnished with the furniture of Poe's time, is now set aside in his honor.

Long before he founded the University of Virginia, Jefferson had been deeply concerned over the lack of opportunities for people to get an education. He believed education was the best foundation that could be devised "for the preservation of our freedom and happiness." Back in 1771 he had proposed to the Virginia legislature a system of primary and secondary schools leading up to a state university. Nearly forty years later the legislature finally caught up with his thinking and appropriated money for educational purposes.

Seeing his opportunity at last, Jefferson obtained a charter for Central College and, with the help of friends, raised $40,000 to purchase the site. Jefferson drew up the plans for his "academical village" and work was started on Pavilion VII on West Lawn. The cornerstone was laid on October 6, 1817, by President Monroe, with Jefferson and Madison looking on.

Next year the Virginia legislature appointed a commission, with Jefferson as its head, to choose a site and develop plans for a state university. There was strong competition for the location of the university but Jefferson persuaded the commission to establish the university on the Central College site, merge with the college and take over the buildings under construction. The University of Virginia was chartered in 1819.

By 1825 the university was ready for the first occupants, and sixty-eight students matriculated on March 7. By the end of the first session, 123 students were enrolled.

Jefferson, who died the year after the university opened, got great satisfaction out of strolling about the grounds and contemplating his handiwork. Sometimes he invited students to dine with him at Monticello. How excited the students must have been at the thought of dining with such a talented, distinguished and interesting host.

But Jefferson's plan of self-government for the students did not work out very well in the beginning. "Censors" selected from the student body failed to function as they should and the faculty did not have authority to act. After much student disorder and rioting, the faculty resigned in October, 1825. Jefferson, deeply upset over the failure of the students to govern themselves, called a meeting of the Board of Visitors, which gave the faculty the right to make and administer rules. And the rules they made were strict. Students were required to wear dull gray uniforms, get up in darkness and attend first classes by candle light, deposit their spending money with the university's business manager for him to parcel out as he saw fit, and hold no parties in their rooms, not even a "little chicken supper," without permission. Friction continued. Students rioted over wearing uniforms in 1831 and publicly horse-whipped the chairman of the faculty in 1839. A year later a masked student shot and mortally wounded a professor, John A. G. Davis, in front of his home at Pavilion X. Nearly all the disorder and trouble had been caused by a few unmanageable students, and most of the students were shocked by the death of the professor. They tried to help capture the murderer but he killed himself.

Out of all this early disorder and friction between students and faculty came one important development. The faculty adopted a rule requiring each student to pledge on his honor that he had no assistance during examinations and had not assisted anyone. The students gradually assumed the responsibility of seeing that no one violated his pledged word and that those who did left the university. Thus the origin of the university's "Honor System."

Enrollment rose to over 600 in the period before the Civil War and other buildings were added to the original "academical village." The most significant was the Annex, or New Hall, a huge, rectangular structure jutting far out from the north side of the Rotunda and drastically altering the majestic, balanced appearance of that building. The Annex was built on a high, terraced base, with tunnels for entrance from the ground level. While it did provide needed classrooms and a public hall seating 1,200, the Annex was completely out of harmony with the perfect proportions of the Rotunda. A fire destroyed the Annex, the dome and inside of the Rotunda in 1895. Fortunately, the Annex was not rebuilt.

Instead, the Rotunda was reconstructed with a north portico where the Annex had been. Two wings were added on the north to match those on the south, with a colonnade in between, forming enclosed courts next to the Rotunda. In the reconstruction of the Rotunda, the second floor was eliminated, adding another sixteen feet in height to the Library Room under the dome. Tall Corinthian columns around the perimeter supported galleries for books. The result was an elegant but rather cold and impersonal area, unlike the original room whose proportions were pleasing and comfortable and whose dome was not so lofty as to be intimidating.

In 1974-76, the interior of the Rotunda was torn out and

restored to look the way Jefferson had designed it, with a first floor as well as a basement, each with three oval rooms, and the big Library Room under the dome. Now you can see it much the way it was in Jefferson's day.

Before the turn of the century, the university still retained something of a rural setting, separated from the town of Charlottesville by farm houses, fields and woods. But that soon changed during the first half of this century as Charlottesville spread past the university and the university added new buildings to take care of the steadily increasing enrollment. For the 1940-41 session, on the eve of World War II, 2,992 students were enrolled.

Then came the postwar flood of students, a large number of them veterans. Over 5,100 students registered for the 1947-48 session, seriously straining the university's facilities until construction could catch up with enrollment.

Restrained but steady growth has continued. By 1977 the number of students had increased to over 15,000. And building has kept pace. But the buildings in recent years, more removed from the central campus, have gone completely modern in design, rather than trying to retain anything of the Jeffersonian look of columns and colonnades. As different as they are from the classical structures at the heart of the campus, these buildings seem to fit together in a functional way.

One of the most radical changes at the university has been the admission of women. Agitation for this began early in this century but made little headway until after World War I. In 1920-21 women were admitted to attend the graduate and professional departments. That's the way it remained for over twenty years. Then, in 1944, when women were taking over men's jobs on the home front and serving in the Armed Forces, the Virginia legislature took a step of appeasement and made Mary Washington (Women's) College in Fredericksburg a division of the university and changed the name to Mary Washington College of the University of Virginia. This was not enough and the university finally gave in and opened the doors to women. Now the student body is about equally divided but the number of women faculty members is proportionately small.

Through the long span of years since it opened, through all the changes these hurrying years have brought, the University of Virginia has maintained a position of eminence in the academic world. And Jefferson's "academical village," where it all started, has been preserved and restored for all to see.

Charlottesville &
Albemarle County

As you drive through the beautiful, rolling countryside of Albemarle County and walk along the streets of historic old Charlottesville, you get a feeling that there is something different about this place.

What makes it different? How did it come about? Not easy questions to answer. But certainly the enduring influence of Thomas Jefferson was strong in creating the personality of the community. And there were the influences of many other people, some whose names are preserved in books and bronze and stone, countless others who served in their own ways and left their names written on the wind. And, of course, the University of Virginia, a pervasive cultural influence coloring the life of the whole community. Then there are the mountains, a subtle but ever-present influence. Mountains are everywhere. Some are so low it is only with kindness that they are ranked above hills. Others are lofty enough to be serenely secure in their mountain status. These are old, old mountains, worn and rounded by the elements; their features are not hard and sharp and aloof like the sky-reaching Rockies, but gentle and softly contoured and friendly.

Even though you may encounter the fumes and frustration of ever-increasing traffic and wince at the garish commercial development along Route 29, you will find much to enjoy on your visit to Charlottesville and Albemarle and you can escape for a while into a less-hurried past as you view historic sites.

Like many other places, Charlottesville and Albemarle have grown vigorously since World War II. This growth has drastically changed the appearance of the area as the city spilled, rather haphazardly, far out into the county. The suburbs have been the focus of all kinds of construction—apartment complexes, shopping centers, office buildings, housing developments, factories, business establishments, restaurants—and it is still in full swing, spreading further and further.

But while all this growth was going on in the suburbs, downtown Charlottesville, once the center of business and commercial activity, was slowly withering away. The central city was suffering from the same ailment that affects so many other—and larger—urban areas: suburbanitis. In a bold, courageous move, perhaps partly in desperation, the city turned five blocks of East Main Street

47

into a pleasant, attractive mall where pedestrians may stroll undisturbed by traffic sounds and smells. The city is gambling that this mall will serve as a catalyst to encourage other improvements and revitalize the downtown area. The new mall is only two blocks from the Court Square, which served long ago as the village green, and the old County Court House, part of which was built in 1803 and is still in use.

The first settlers in Albemarle County arrived about 1727. Hunters and explorers had visited the county before that time and some had even built crude cabins. But none had obtained a grant of land and settled down.

There seems to have been little trouble with the Indians and most of them had moved on westward before the arrival of the first settlers. A tribe of Indians called the Monacans once had a town on the south branch of the Rivanna River a few miles north of where Charlottesville was built. By an interesting coincidence, the unpronounceable name of that Indian town—Monasukapanough—has the same number of letters as Charlottesville.

Albemarle County was named for the Earl of Albemarle, who was governor of the Virginia colony from 1737 to 1754 but who was never interested enough to make the long trip to this country, probably thinking it was much too primitive. Albemarle was originally a huge county. As more settlers

moved into the area, they wanted a center of government nearer to their homes so they could reach it easier on foot or horseback over the rough trails and roads. Five whole counties, plus parts of two others, were lopped off Albemarle, leaving the boundaries about the way they are today.

The county seat for Albemarle was first located at Scott's Landing, now

Scottsville, where Samuel Scott owned land and operated a ferry across the James River and where a small cable ferry still operates today at Hatton, a short distance from Scottsville. Since Scott's Landing was on the far southeastern edge of Albemarle, settlers sought a new seat of government that would be closer to the center of the county. In response, the Virginia legislature in 1762 created the town of Charlottesville, named in honor of England's Queen Charlotte, young wife of King George III. The original town consisted of fifty acres of land laid out in lots and streets, with the focal point the Court Square, where a frame court house, whipping post, pillory and stocks were built for proper and visible enforcement of the laws of the land.

Farming was the principal occupation in those days and the town existed largely to supply the needs of the surrounding farms. Most of the early settlers in Albemarle came looking for land on which to grow tobacco, the big money crop in Colonial Virginia. Although a considerable amount of this pungent weed was grown in Albemarle, it is a greedy crop that robs the soil of its nutrients and productivity, and farmers began to diversify and devote more land to grains, cattle and fruit. They found the soil and climate well suited to apples, peaches, cherries and other fruits. Orchards spread over the hills and mountainsides and in the springtime the blossoming trees splashed the greening countryside with great masses of delicate pink and white.

One apple, the delicious Albemarle pippin, brought far-spread recognition to the county's products. Queen Victoria of England received a gift basket of the apples in 1838 and liked their taste so well that barrels of the pippins were shipped to Britian's royal family each harvest season for many years.

Until recent years, Albemarle was one of the top apple producing counties and grew more peaches than any other area in the state. While fruit growing has declined, raising horses and beef cattle remains quite popular. You can see chunky black Angus cattle converting grassy pastures into prime beef and you can watch sleek horses grazing behind

the white board fences of big estates. You can be sure the long tradition of gentlemen farmers is still alive and flourishing in Albemarle. On a frosty autumn morning you may hear the quaint and urgent sound of a horn summoning red-coated riders and listen to the baying of the hounds as they pursue a hapless fox.

Most visitors come here to see Monticello, the University of Virginia and other historic places. You will also find it well worth your time—even as scarce and precious as time is these days—to drive along some of the roads leading out of the city. There are quite a few beautiful estates and much of the land is still covered by forests. You will be rewarded with many pleasing scenes as you follow the winding roads up and down across the landscape.

Thomas Jefferson, who expressed himself with great enthusiasm whenever he referred to the land he loved, once wrote:

"The situation of Charlottesville is in a mountainous, healthy, fertile country, delicious climate, good water, cheap subsistence, an independent yeomanry, many wealthy persons, good society, and free as air in religion and politics."

Surely after nearly 200 years, years of tremendous change, you would expect such a statement to need revision. Neither subsistence nor anything else is "cheap" any more. But, once you've had a chance to look around, you may agree that Mr. Jefferson's description is surprisingly accurate today.

Ash Lawn

A "CABIN CASTLE" was the way James Monroe described the simple three-room cottage he built in the high country of Albemarle County about two miles from the home of his good friend, Thomas Jefferson.

The "cabin castle" is hidden behind a larger, more imposing two-story addition built onto the cottage in 1862 by John E. Massey, owner at the time. This addition, with a portico added in 1930, serves as the "front" of the house, the part you will see first as you approach along a walkway lined with old boxwood that has grown into a massive hedge. Monroe himself expanded the original cottage by adding a room where a porch may have been and building other rooms in front where the two-story Massey addition now stands.

Monroe called his home "Highland," not "Ash Lawn," as it is known today. You can guess why John Massey changed the name when you see the big ash trees shading the lawn. Perhaps its present owner, the College of William and Mary, will restore the original name, along with the other careful restoration it is undertaking. "Highland" is a much more seemly name for a "cabin castle."

Don't be startled if you hear a loud, unearthly scream as you approach the house. It's only the cry of one of the resident peacocks roaming the lawn. Though it is unlikely they will replace the faithful watchdog, peacocks are supposed to be excellent at announcing the presence of strangers. To little children, the peacocks may be the most interesting feature of the home. Children's eyes open wide at their first glimpse of these big, exotic fowl, especially the proud males strutting around in their resplendent plumage. You can buy a small bag of peacock food in the home but, like too many of us, the peacocks seem a trifle overfed.

Your tour of the house starts in the entrance hall under the guidance of a well-informed hostess who will tell you briefly of Monroe's life and then conduct you through the connecting cottage where Monroe lived. As you proceed through the small rooms of the cottage, you will see interesting period pieces and some things owned by the Monroes, reflecting their liking for French furniture, a taste acquired while he served as Minister to France under his friend, President Madison.

You will have to walk through a chimney on your way out of the house. Monroe built a very low, arched passageway right through the middle of a tremendously thick and wide chimney.

The tour ends in the basement kitchen, where the big fireplace was once used for cooking. You can see such period items as an old waffle iron that cooked four small waffles, each with a different pattern, and a "toe toaster," not, as you might think, used to warm feet, but made with a revolving bread holder that enabled the user to turn it with the toe of her shoe so the fire could toast both sides.

After the house tour you may wish to stroll about the lawns and breathe the clean, fresh air of this still rural area of pastures and woods. You can see the statue of Monroe chiseled by the same sculptor, Attilio Piccirilli, who created the bust of Monroe in the entrance hallway of the house. Sometimes you can see a weaver working at an old fashioned loom and watch a blacksmith shaping iron on an anvil.

James Monroe attended the College of William and Mary and, after serving in the Revolutionary War, studied law under Jefferson. As is often the case, law became a pathway to political office. He served as Governor of Virginia, United States Senator, Secretary of State and War, Minister to France, Minister to England and President of the United States.

To be near Jefferson, Monroe bought a place close to the village of Charlottesville. (This place, Monroe Hill, is now a part of the University of Virginia.) Later he purchased the land where he built Highland, fulfilling a wish he expressed to Jefferson in a letter: "It has always been my wish to acquire property near Monticello."

This close friendship between the two men ended only with Jefferson's death. Both men died on Independence Day, Jefferson on July 4, 1826, and Monroe on July 4, 1841. And both men died deeply in debt. Public service was not as remunerative then as it is today.

Michie Tavern

WHEN "Scotch John" Michie bought a home in northern Albemarle County in 1746 and later turned it into a thriving tavern, he couldn't have had the faintest idea his place would wind up one day as a charming museum on the road up Monticello Mountain.

Michie Tavern was moved in 1927 from its original location to its present site. Today it stands, restored and furnished with period pieces, much the way it was when "Scotch John" and later on his son, William, kept this popular wayside inn.

The tavern was built around 1735 as a home by John Henry, the father of Patrick Henry. A few years after Henry built the house, John Michie, who had come to this country from Scotland, bought the building and a thousand acres of land. "Scotch John" gradually turned it into a tavern to serve people traveling a road that passed near the house. The tavern was a stopping place for many famous people in its early days, including Jefferson, Madison, Monroe, General Lafayette and General Jackson.

You step back in time when you walk into the tavern museum. And how prim and polite the names of the rooms

55

sound—gentlemen's parlor, ladies' parlor, the ballroom and eating parlor. A recorded voice tells you about the authentic period furnishings of the rooms—canopied beds, foot-warmers, 1780 hoop skirt, revolving candles, Mr. Michie's pipe and spectacles, settler's table that tilts up to form a bench, William Michie's flint lock rifle, and many other items. That daring dance, the round dance or waltz, was supposed to have been first performed in this country in the ballroom, much to the shocked disapproval of some of those present.

Outside, at the back of the tavern, you can visit reproductions of a Colonial privy, spring house, kitchen and smoke house. And in the wine cellar you can read the rules of the tavern, which remind you how different life was in those days. You could spend the night for four pence and get supper for only two pence more. But, if you were a man, you might have a crowded night. The rule of the men's sleeping room was that no more than five could share a bed. And you absolutely could not wear your boots to bed.

The ordinary, a converted log cabin used as slave quarters long ago, is attached to the tavern. At the ordinary you can sample food similar to that of Colonial days (but prepared in a modern kitchen)—black-eyed peas, stewed tomatoes, curd cheese, cole slaw, green bean salad, corn bread, biscuits, potato salad and fried chicken.

While visiting the tavern, you will find it worth the time to stop by the old mill at the lower end of the parking area. The huge old mill wheel still turns, except in freezing winter weather, but the mill ceased operations years ago. For good luck, you can toss a coin over your shoulder at the big wheel and if you're especially lucky, it will land in one of the "buckets" that help turn the wheel when full of water.

"Scotch John" Michie built such a mill upon his property some two hundred years ago. That mill rotted and disappeared and the mill you see today is the Meadow Run Mill, which was built later in the eighteenth century and was in operation until 1958. This mill, thought to resemble Michie's mill, was moved piece by piece from its location at Laurel Hill, Virginia, fifty miles away, and put back together again at its present site. Moving and reconstructing the mill took two and a half years.

Legends grow up like weeds about places like old mills, and the Meadow Run Mill has its share. The most romantic is the tale of the miller's daughter, a lovely maiden who was in love with the miller's young apprentice. The miller did not approve, so the young lovers met secretly at night. She stood on a balcony over the big mill wheel and flashed a shiny silver coin in the moonlight, and her lover, waiting on the other side of the mill stream, would flash another coin in reply. The maiden would stop the mill wheel from turning by wedging a piece of wood between the wheel and the wall. Then the young apprentice would climb up the mill wheel to her.

But one night the wooden wedge slipped as the apprentice was climbing up and the wheel began to turn. The maiden grabbed her lover's hand and they were both thrown into the water. Whether they escaped or drowned is not known, but, as is often the case with such romantic tales, there's a ghostly sequel. When the moon rides high in the sky at night and the wind sighs and moans through the trees, you can sometimes catch a glimpse of two silver coins flashing in the darkness and hear the muted cries of the young lovers.

Castle Hill

CASTLE HILL has a dual personality. The original house, a frame structure, with wood shingle roof and clapboard siding, was built around 1765 by Dr. Thomas Walker, physician, gentleman farmer, explorer, land speculator and one of the most prominent citizens of the young county. Perhaps reflecting his penchant for exploration, Dr. Walker's home faced westward, looking up toward Walnut Mountain at the back of his property.

Dr. Walker's granddaughter, Judith, inherited the house and more than 3,000 acres of land. She and her husband, William Cabell Rives, felt they needed a home more in keeping with their position in life. Around 1824, they added to the old frame house an imposing brick mansion facing in the opposite direction.

Dr. Walker's plantation at one time contained more than 15,000 acres. With all the slave quarters and outbuildings—smokehouses, springhouse, kitchen, ice house, barns and numerous other "dependencies"—the plantation was actually a small, self-sufficient village. Some of the outbuildings have been preserved and restored. After your tour of the house you can look at these buildings. And the terraced gardens, broad lawns, huge shade trees and old boxwood create a lovely, peaceful scene that invites one to take a leisurely stroll.

Dr. Walker, who was a friend of Peter Jefferson, served as a guardian of young Thomas Jefferson after his father died. He later became a strong political supporter of Jefferson in the period leading up to the Revolution.

Castle Hill was owned by members of the Walker-Rives family until 1947 and is now owned by Mr. and Mrs. Don-Michael Bird. It was the residence of Prince Pierre Troubetzkoy and his wife, Amele Rives, a writer whose novels included "The Quick or the Dead."

George Rogers Clark Museum

A VISIT to the George Rogers Clark Museum will give you a glimpse of how the less affluent lived in the early days of Albemarle County.

The simple log cabin housing the museum was built about 1740 and was originally located fifteen miles away from its present site. Since this log house was thought to be similar to George Rogers Clark's childhood home, it was carefully moved piece by piece, to the place where Clark was born. It was reconstructed here along the Rivanna River a little over a mile from Charlottesville on Stony Point Road (Route 20). The house is now open to the public as a museum, filled with furniture, china and utensils from long ago.

The place is especially interesting because it is a rare specimen of the log cabins of its time. Brick and frame houses of the

more affluent have been preserved but very, very few of the simple log houses have survived wind, rain, decay and neglect for more than two hundred years. The crude appearance and cramped quarters of these houses inspired little desire to preserve them.

Clark's actual birthplace disappeared long ago. He was born November 19, 1752. Nothing remained to indicate the site but a pile of rocks. The log house museum was reconstructed on that site.

The three-room house was built of logs cut from the virgin forests covering much of Albemarle County in those days. The logs were hewn and notched and fitted together and the cracks between them were chinked with red clay. During the reconstruction, a small amount of cement and sand was mixed with red clay mud to give the substance more permanence.

The original floors of the cabin are heart pine boards, an inch thick and six, ten and twelve inches wide. People were not as tall then as today, and the ceilings of the cabin are quite low. The cabin has one central chimney, with fireplaces in the living room, upstairs bedroom and the kitchen, where it was used for cooking as well as for heat.

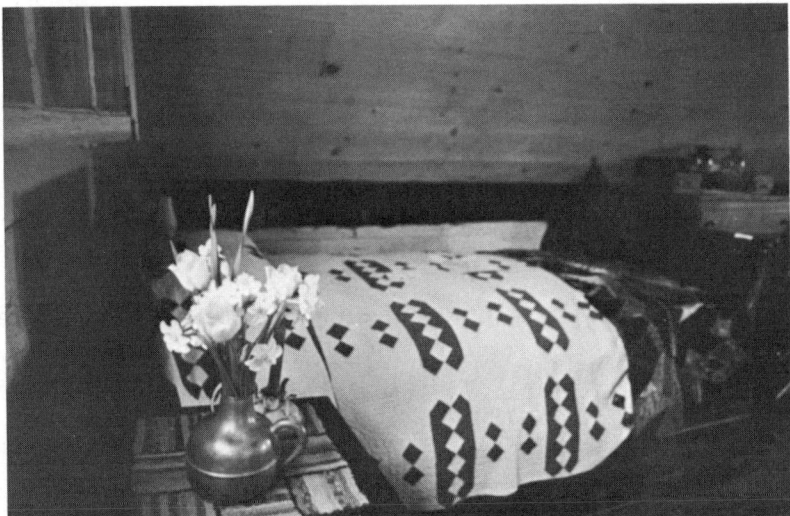

Clark's family moved from their Albemarle County farm when he was five years old and settled on a small plantation a hundred miles east in Caroline County. As a youngster, he received some schooling but his heart was not in it. He was more interested in exciting tales of the frontier and the wilderness land beyond the mountains. Later he made several trips into the country along the Ohio River and settled on rich bottom land in what is now Kentucky.

In 1776 Clark and a companion walked nearly five hundred miles from Kentucky to Williamsburg and then to Governor Patrick Henry's home in Hanover County to try to talk to the Virginia leaders. They wanted to persuade them to make Kentucky a part of Virginia and to give the people there military help against an expected attack by the British. The trip was successful. Kentucky was made a county of Virginia. Clark was appointed a lieutenant-colonel in the Virginia militia and authorized to raise a force to attack the British fort at

Kaskaskia (Illinois). With less than two hundred men, Clark surprised and captured the fort.

He later took the British fort at Vincennes (Indiana) but his forces were spread very thin and he could leave only a handful of men to defend it. The British took this opportunity to recapture the fort. Clark, who was at Kaskaskia, heard of the recapture and immediately began planning an attack. It was the middle of winter and Vincennes was over two hundred miles away across flooded prairies. Most men would have said it couldn't be done. Not the stubborn, red-headed Clark. Setting an example by plunging ahead when the going was toughest, Clark led his men on an almost unbelievable march, sometimes wading all day through icy water, which at times came up to their shoulders. The indomitable Clark encouraged, cajoled and threatened his men to keep them going when they felt they could not possibly drag themselves any further. They reached the fort to the surprise and amazement of the British general and captured it after a short siege.

Clark's determined campaign against the British won for the United States the vast Northwest Territory, from which five states were later formed—Illinois, Wisconsin, Michigan, Indiana and Ohio.

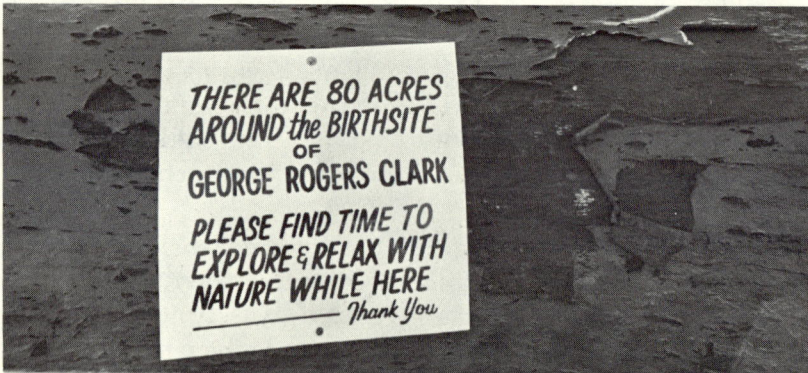

THERE ARE 80 ACRES AROUND the BIRTHSITE OF GEORGE ROGERS CLARK PLEASE FIND TIME TO EXPLORE & RELAX WITH NATURE WHILE HERE — Thank You

Jack Jouett

The Man Who Outrode Paul Revere

JACK JOUETT? Ever heard of him? Not many people have. He is an almost unknown hero of the American Revolutionary War.

Yet Jouett's gruelling, dramatic night ride to prevent the British capture of Governor Thomas Jefferson and the members of the Virginia Legislature surpassed the ride of Paul Revere in every way—except in the vast publicity Revere's ride has received.

Jack Jouett's ride of over forty miles was about four times the distance, much more difficult and daring and of greater importance to the fortunes of the Revolution.

Paul Revere rode two or three hours along a main highway.

Jack Jouett rode all night long across the rough, hilly, heavily-forested countryside of central Virginia—along trails and paths, across fields and streams, through forest and brush.

An almost full moon aided Jouett in finding his way through the woods and thickets. For the rest of his life, however, his face bore deep scars left by the slashing tree branches.

In contrast, Paul Revere, riding with a companion, William Dawes, covered some ten miles on the highway from Boston to Lexington. Neither man ever got to Concord, their planned destination.

They warned Samuel Adams and John Hancock in Lexington. Then Revere, Dawes and Dr. Samuel Prescott started out for Concord. But they were intercepted by a British Cavalry detachment and Revere was captured. Only Dr. Prescott got through to Concord.

Jack Jouett rode alone. He spotted the British troopers as they rode past Cuckoo Tavern in Louisa County, Virginia, around 10 o'clock on the night of June 3, 1781. He quietly mounted his horse and galloped off across the countryside to try to reach Charlottesville before the British.

Fortunately, Jouett was familiar with the country. He lived in Charlottesville, where his father ran a tavern, and he had been visiting his father's farm in Louisa.

Jouett, twenty-seven, was a big, powerful man. He and his three brothers were captains in the Virginia militia and one brother had been killed at the battle of Brandywine. And Jack Jouett rode a horse that, according to one account, was "the best and fleetest of foot of any nag in seven counties."

It was about 4:30 in the morning when Jouett finally rode up to Thomas Jefferson's home, Monticello. He awakened Governor Jefferson and his guests, who included several members of the Virginia legislature. Then he rode on to the town of Charlottesville, where the legislature had fled when the British threatened Richmond, the state capital.

The British dragoons, under Colonel Banastre Tarleton, rode into town on the heels of the last of the fleeing legislators and managed to capture several of them. One of those captured, Daniel Boone, reportedly spent an uncomfortable night as a prisoner in a coal cellar before he was paroled the next day. Boone, a well-known frontiersman, was a member of the legislature from the territory that is now the State of Kentucky but was then a part of Virginia.

General Edward Stevens, who was recovering from a

wound suffered in the Battle of Guilford Court House three months earlier, was almost captured. The British troopers spotted General Stevens and Jack Jouett as they were riding out of town. General Stevens was plainly dressed and riding an unimpressive horse. Jouett, riding his beautiful thorough-bred mare, was dressed in a military hat and a bright scarlet coat he loved to wear. The British rode in pursuit of Jouett. But he was too fast for them and escaped, as did General Stevens.

If the British had captured Governor Jefferson, author of the Declaration of Independence, and important members of the Virginia legislature, it would have been a shocking blow. Things were not going well for the Americans and morale was low. Jouett's daring ride foiled a clever British maneuver that could have had a serious effect on the Revolution.

Jack Jouett?

Bicentennial Center

THE Western Virginia Bicentennial Center will help you get your bearings. If you want to know how to get somewhere or what activities are currently taking place, this is the handiest place to go. Travel counselors will provide information and brochures on hundreds of points of interest in Virginia, as well as Charlottesville.

And if you need motel reservations anywhere in Virginia, the Bicentennial Center will make them for you free of charge.

In addition to the information center, you'll find a gift shop and exhibits. Don't miss the exhibits. The focus is on Western Virginia—colonial explorations and pioneer settlements.

There's also an interesting film, "Mr. Jefferson's Legacy," narrated by Earl Hamner, Jr., creator of *The Waltons,* who grew up near Charlottesville.

The Bicentennial Center is on Route 20 South, just south of the I-64 exit. (The center is on the way to Monticello.) Hours are 9 A.M. to 5 P.M., and there is no admission fee.

A Walk Around
The University

WALKING tours of the University of Virginia are conducted regularly from the Rotunda during most of the year. The student guides are quite knowledgeable and are prepared to answer questions. If, however, you want to set your own pace, then you may wish to take the tour we have outlined. This walk takes you through Thomas Jefferson's "academical village," the name he gave to the original buildings of the university. The arrangement of the buildings does have something of the appearance of a village, but an unusual one, and surely more beautiful than most any other village you'll ever see. Jefferson designed every one of the original buildings, even the smallest detail, and he personally supervised every phase of the construction. His architectural genius is evident everywhere but it reaches a magnificent peak in his creation of the Rotunda.

The Rotunda is the focal point of the "academical village." So let's begin our tour there.

Jefferson designed the Rotunda as a half-size replica of the Pantheon in Rome. It is 77 feet in diameter and in height, with a dome of 120 degrees. From whatever direction you approach the Rotunda you can see its serene, classic beauty crowning the highest point on the campus, but it is perhaps most impressive when viewed from the Lawn. This is also the easiest side to photograph.

If you stand some distance away from the Rotunda, you can get a better idea of its over-all design and the way it fits so flawlessly into the setting. Walk up the steps to the portico

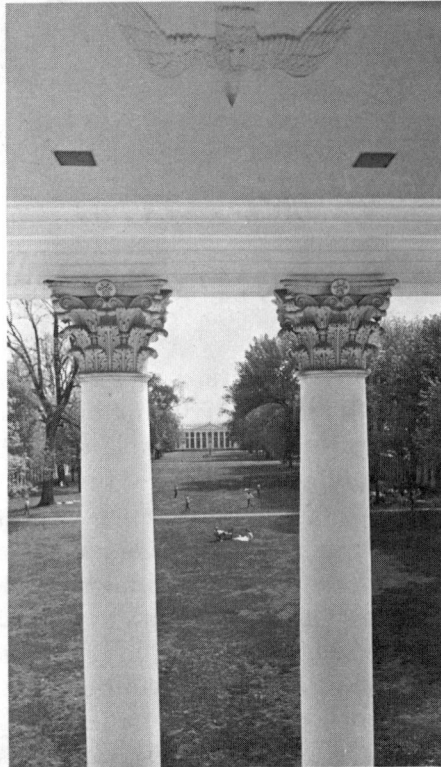

and turn and look out upon the Lawn. This is a lovely vista, with the broad, tree-edged Lawn stretching for some 600 feet, in long, grassy terraces to Cabell Hall at the other end. The main section of Cabell Hall was completed in 1899 and was not a part of Jefferson's original plan. Jefferson had envisioned the Lawn continuing on and other buildings added along the sides as needed.

Standing here you can get a good view of the layout of the place. On each side of the Lawn—called East Lawn and West Lawn—are five two-story houses of classic proportions and style. (Jefferson called them "pavilions.") These were—and all but two still are—the homes of professors. Between these houses are rows of one-story student rooms. And along the front of the houses and student rooms runs a low colonnade, providing a sturdy, charming passageway protected from the weather but from which you can see the Lawn through the arches.

Walk back down the steps and along the brick walkway leading to either side of the Lawn. A short flight of steps will take you down to the arcade leading to the Rotunda basement. Once inside, you will see that both the basement and the main

floor contain three oval rooms fitted into the circular shape of the Rotunda. Probably you will find the rooms on the main floor more interesting than those in the basement. These rooms are beautifully decorated and furnished and there are interesting touches, such as the gleaming, highly-polished brass chandeliers and a huge oval table in the Board Room. A bust of Jefferson presides with solemn dignity in the room that looks out on the north portico. And in the central hall is a full size statue of Jefferson, sculpted by Alexander Galt.

Students saved this statue by carrying it out in blankets when fire destroyed all but the outer walls of the Rotunda in 1895.

When you go up the stairs to the top floor, you may stop and stare in wonder as you see for the first time the perfect proportions that make this vast and lofty Dome Room seem magnificent and yet pleasant and friendly. The skylight at the top of the dome and the windows around the room combine to give a bright and cheerful look to a room that could have been gloomy. Alcoves with bookcases filled with old books are tucked away behind paired columns that encircle the room, a reminder that this room originally served as the library as well as a center for social events. Jefferson apparently had a fondness for dome rooms since they are distinctive features of both Monticello and the Rotunda.

When you leave the Rotunda, walk to the right to the colonnade along West Lawn. As you walk down this colonnade, you will see that each one of the two-story, columned pavilions is different in appearance and represents a different style of architecture. Jefferson designed them that way so they could be used as architectural specimens by the professors in their lectures. Pavilion VII toward the end of West Lawn was the first building of the university. The cornerstone was laid October 6, 1817, by President Monroe. This pavilion now houses the Colonnade Club, a social club for faculty members, administrative officials and alumni.

If you happen to be visiting the university during the cooler months, you will notice the firewood stacked in front of the student rooms along the colonnade and you may catch the pungent smell of wood burning in the fireplaces.

Continue on when you reach the end of the colonnade and you will see a seated statue of Jefferson, set back from the walkway in a tiny garden. And if you care to cross the Lawn to the other side, you can see a replica of Houdon's statue of Washington.

Cabell Hall, with an auditorium, classrooms and academic offices, closes in the southern end of the Lawn. A statue of Homer and His Young Guide stands in the center of the Lawn in front of Cabell Hall.

Back of the buildings of East Lawn and West Lawn are large, walled gardens designed by Jefferson to provide food for the professors who lived in the pavilions. They were used as vegetable gardens and as places for the professors to keep their horses, cows and pigs. The gardens were reconstructed in a formal design by the Garden Club of Virginia. Reconstruction included restoration of the graceful serpentine walls, which are not only beautiful but functional, their curving lines making it possible to build a sturdy wall only one brick thick. You can visit these gardens but keep in mind that they are the backyards of the professors living in the pavilions.

Pavilion IX, the last one on the West Lawn, was once the home of Professor William H. McGuffey, who joined the university faculty in 1845 and gained widespread recognition for his famous McGuffey Readers. Over 122 million copies of these readers were sold and untold millions of school children learned to read with the help of these books. Legend has it that Professor McGuffey, when working on a book, often tested some of the passages at children's parties held under a giant ash tree in the pavilion garden. This enormous, beautifully shaped tree towers over the garden today and is called "McGuffey's Ash."

The pavilion gardens, divided into two sections, extend about 300 feet to rows of student rooms called the Ranges. East Range and West Range run parallel to East Lawn and West Lawn and have colonnades similar to those on the Lawns. But instead of pavilions, the Ranges have "hotels," three of them to each Range, equally spaced between the student rooms. The hotels were orginally used as dining rooms for the students but are now used as offices and meeting rooms.

If you walk north along the colonnade of West Range to Room 13, you will have an opportunity to get some idea of the appearance of the student rooms. Number 13 West Range was occupied for one session by Edgar Allan Poe, probably the most famous of the students at the university in the early years. The room was set aside as a memorial to Poe and furnished as it might have been in his day. Visitors are permitted to look into the room through the door but are not allowed to enter the room.

When you reach the northern end of the colonnade for West Range, you leave Jefferson's "academical village" and walk north towards the University Chapel, a gothic structure built in 1872 and quite different in style from Jefferson's classic architecture. The chapel is now rarely used except to chime the hours and for weddings and funerals.

On your left as you face the chapel is Alderman Library. It was built with a grant from the Public Works Administration

and opened in 1938. It has been enlarged twice since then. In addition to being an outstanding academic library, it also houses a fine collection of rare books and manuscripts.

To the west of the library, "Soaring Like an Eagle, into New Heavens of Valor and Devotion," is the "Aviator," a statue by Gutzon Borglum. It was given to the university in memory of James Rogers McConnell, an alumnus killed in World War I.

Continue on past the chapel across the campus and you will get another good view of the Rotunda, this time from the north side. You can see a statue of Jefferson on an esplanade in front of two broad flights of steps leading up to the portico of the Rotunda. Jefferson stands on a replica of the Liberty Bell. Surrounding the bell are four figures—Liberty, Justice, Religious Freedom and Human Freedom—that represent the ideals Jefferson devoted much of his life to. The sculptor, Sir Moses Ezekiel, cast the statue in Rome and presented it to the State of Virginia.

The esplanade where the statue stands is part of the foundation left when a building called the Annex was destroyed by fire in 1895. The Annex was an ungainly rectangular structure that thrust itself far out from the Rotunda. It was added to the Rotunda in 1853 and must have caused Jefferson to stir resentfully in his grave. The fire gutted both the Annex and the Rotunda but the Annex wisely was not rebuilt.

Only the brick walls of the Rotunda remained after the fire. When it was rebuilt the interior was changed drastically. Architect Stanford White combined the top floor and main floor into one huge Library Room with big columns. He also added the north portico you now see and two wings on the north to go with the original wings. The Rotunda remained that way for three-quarters of a century until the interior was restored in 1976 to look much as it did in Jefferson's day.

Now that this walking tour of the university is completed, you may wish to continue on across the campus to University Avenue and "The Corner," where for many generations students have gathered for conversation and refreshment. And if you're interested in going deeper into the history of the university, then we recommend you consider "Pictorial History of the University of Virginia," available at book stores on University Avenue. This book by William B. O'Neal is well written, complete and full of photographs.

A Walk Around
Old Charlottesville

THIS walking tour will take you through the historic old
section of Charlottesville, where Jefferson, Madison and
Monroe walked together on the Court Square, where equestrian statues of Civil War heroes keep their bronze watch in
quiet little parks, and where a new "people's mall" has
changed five time-weathered blocks of Main Street into a

A Walk Around Old Charlottesville

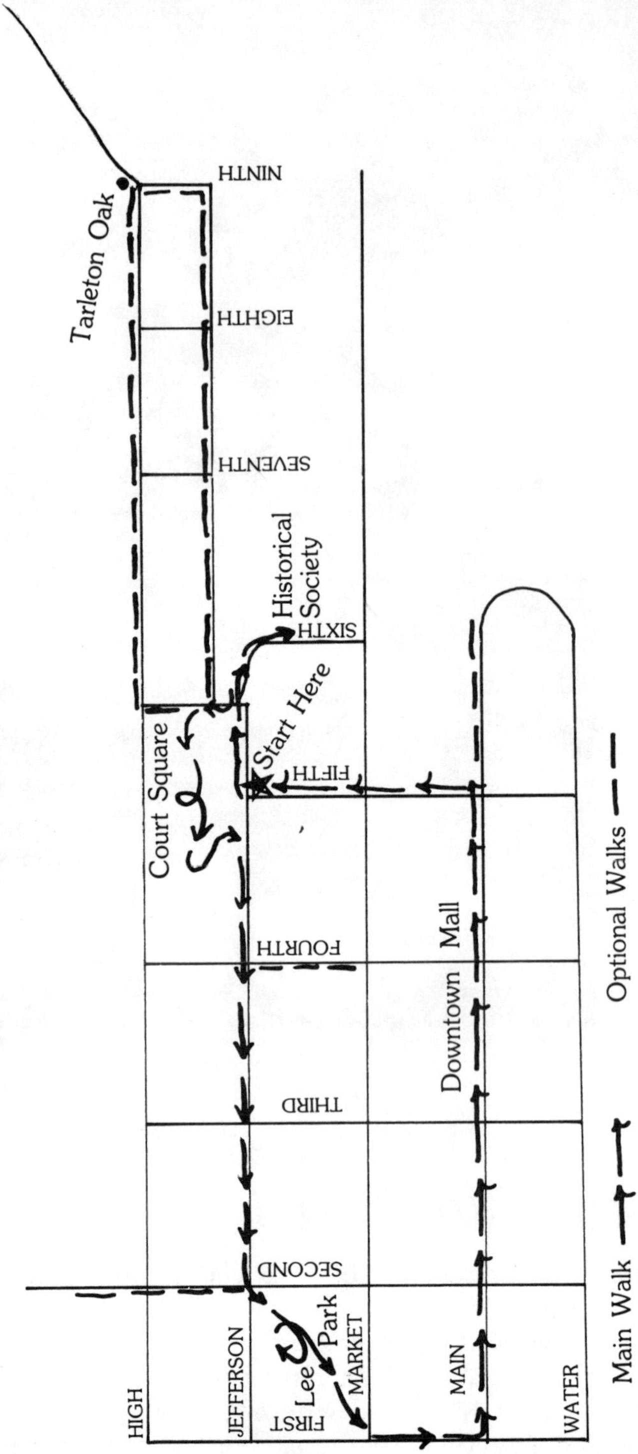

NINTH

Tarleton Oak

EIGHTH

SEVENTH

Historical
Society

SIXTH

Court Square

Start Here

FIFTH

FOURTH

Downtown Mall

THIRD

SECOND

HIGH

JEFFERSON

Lee Park

FIRST

MARKET

MAIN

WATER

Main Walk

Optional Walks

82

pleasant avenue that restores joy to strolling, shopping or pausing nostalgically for an ice cream soda.

A good place to begin your walking tour of Charlottesville is across from Court Square at Fifth (Court) and Jefferson Streets. The present building opened in 1926 as the Monticello Hotel, a luxurious hotel that owed much in its decor to Jefferson's Monticello.

Perhaps the oddest reason for the Monticello Hotel's fame in the late 1920's was a giant searchlight on the hotel's roof. The brilliant beam swept slowly across the sky from the University of Virginia to Monticello, back and forth, back and forth, three hours a night, several months each year. This 1.2 billion candlepower searchlight was then the largest in the world; its beam was visible for 300 miles and was reportedly seen as far away as South Carolina.

For over two centuries this block has been a place for dining, entertaining and lodging. Although the hotel has been converted into private residences and is now called Court Square Condominium, the Monticello Room (upstairs) and the Court Square Tavern (downstairs) are open to the public and make fine places to begin or end your walk. (Lunch upstairs; snacks, light meals and sandwiches, "refreshing beverages" downstairs.)

The section of the building at Sixth and Jefferson is considerably older, dating from the mid 1800's. By 1791, a two-and-a-half story, wooden tavern was located here. Known at the Eagle Tavern, it was apparently the center of much of Charlottesville's social and business activity. Public dances and political celebrations were held here. Merchants sold their goods from the front porch. One revivalist minister railed about the immorality of the place, and at another time as many as 200 people dined at one meal while their horses were tended to and fed in the nearby stables. The Eagle Tavern was replaced by the present brick building. Known as Farish House, it continued serving as Charlottesville's main inn.

Sixth Steeet was the eastern boundary of the village of Charlottesville. Cross Sixth and turn right. The last building before the alley, at 220 Court Square, is Albemarle County Historical Society Library and Museum. In 1811 John Yeargain built on this site a "fine liquor" store. Legend has it that he was a miser who hoarded gold in his basement. Today genealogists find the library downstairs a goldmine of information. Practically everyone, it seems, can trace back to Albemarle a wispy family root. And the ladies from the Historical Society are very helpful and gracious in lending assistance.

Library Hours: Tues. 10 A.M. - 12:30 P.M.
Wed. 10 A.M. - Noon, 1 - 4 P.M.
Thurs. 1 - 4:30 P.M.
Fri. Noon - 4:30 P.M.
Also by appointment

Museum Hours: Tues. - Wed. 10 A.M. - Noon
Thurs. 2 - 4 P.M.
Fri. (summer) 2 - 4 P.M.
Groups by appointment

As you walk back along Sixth Street to Jefferson, notice the small slate plaques attached to buildings of historic interest. These plaques tell you what was originally on the site and when it was built. It is important to realize that the present buildings are, in most cases, neither originals nor restorations. Many of the old buildings were of wood and have been replaced, sometime along the way, with more permanent structures. Others, such as Farish House, are originals, although generally modified, and usually date from the mid-1800's.

Next to the Historical Society, at 221 Court Square, is the site of the watchmaker's shop. Lewis Leschot settled in Charlottesville in the early nineteenth century as the "resident

84

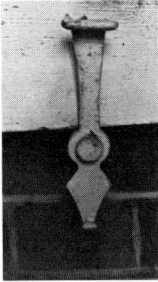

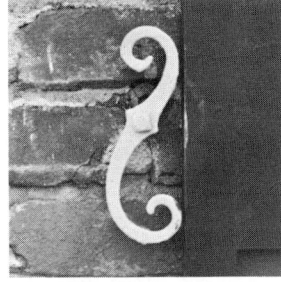

Swiss jeweler," part of Mr. Jefferson's plan to fill the town with skilled and talented foreign craftsmen who could labor here and train others. Surely, Jefferson figured, it was more efficient and productive to import artisans than artifacts.

The site of Charlottesville's first public library is next door at 222 Court Square. It was originally a small frame structure with only one room. Jefferson contributed many books to the library, some of which are preserved today at the University of Virginia's Alderman Library.

In 1815 a store was built on the site that is now 223 Court Square.

On the corner of Sixth and Jefferson is an original building dating from 1820. It was first used as a double store, with each store owned and operated separately from the other. The address was "Number Nothing." Because the space was originally intended for use as a lot for keeping horses, other lots were numbered consecutively. As no appropriate number was available when the horse lot was built upon, it was simply called Number Nothing.

As you walk around old Charlottesville, take note of the small, ornamental iron fixtures next to the shutters. Shutters were not nailed to outside walls merely as decoration. In summer, windows could be opened and shutters closed to allow fresh air and privacy. And in winter, closed shutters kept in heat and protected the house from wind and snow. At other times these iron fixtures kept the shutters open by fastening them to the outside wall. Throughout Charlottesville you'll notice different styles of fasteners—simple twists, elegant shell patterns and ornate floral designs.

Turn the corner from Sixth onto East Jefferson. At the corner of Seventh Street you'll notice a tree with an entwined double trunk. In spring it is a mass of blossoms. Of this tree has grown a remarkable, and probably apocraphyl, legend—a Southern gothic tale of romance and unrequited love early in this century.

It seems the daughter of a wealthy and socially prominent Charlottesville family fell in love with a penniless university student. Her family insisted that she reject him and made plans for her to visit her cousins in Charleston, where she might forget her love and find a more acceptable match.

She dutifully told her lover that she was leaving the next morning and she must see him no more. He honorably accepted her rejection but said he would never marry as long as there was a chance she might change her mind.

Later that day she sent him a message explaining the situation and asking him, if he loved her, to come to her window and rescue her that night so they might elope. Unbeknownst to her, the letter was intercepted by a jealous office boy who worked for her father. And so the girl waited all night by the window for her lover. With resignation she left the next morning for Charleston.

A good match was found for her and two summers later she returned to Charlottesville for her wedding. A year thereafter the young scholar-lawyer also married. He settled in Charlottesville and became prosperous, but an aura of mystery and sadness surrounded him. Always he seemed a little sad.

After her husband's death, she and her children returned to Charlottesville. Everyone attributed her sadness to her mourning.

Their children played together. Her son and his daughter fell in love. And on the spring night of their children's wedding, the former lovers confessed their passion. He placed in her hair blossoms from a flowering tree. And here, where their tears fell, grew up this entwined tree—the lover's tree.

> "Young we loved and were silent,
> And now are full of tears."

This walk along Jefferson is especially pretty in Spring when the warm air is heavy with the scent of flowering trees. Or on a fall day when dry leaves swirl around your feet and autumnal sadness nips at your mood like the bite of the chill wind.

As is much of old Charlottesville, many of the homes here are being restored and revitalized, often as offices. The Carter-Gilmer House at 1802 East Jefferson is a good example of the architecture of the 1820's. Notice that is has four stories and interesting ironwork. And notice also the small bricks that were typical of the period.

At Ninth and Jefferson turn left and go to the Exxon station. The huge gnarled, twisted and patched tree is known as "Tarleton Oak" because it was here that British cavalryman

Banastre Tarleton is said to have camped on his raid on Charlottesville, June 4, 1781. He was foiled by Captain Jack Jouett, who rode through the night by a different route and succeeded in warning the partiots of Tarleton's approach.

Time was when trees this size were common in Virginia. With its twenty-one foot waistline, old Tarleton Oak is now a very rare specimen.

Return to Court Square by High Street. As you walk along the streets of old Charlottesville, you'll often notice the Jeffersonian-classical influence. At the corner of Seventh and High, for instance, you'll see the combination of columns and Chippendalesque railings.

Back at Court Square, at the corner of Sixth and High, is the old Town Hall, which was built in 1851. It later became the Levy Opera House and is currently being restored.

The next building on Sixth is now the Redland Club, a private club for men. The famous Swan Tavern was once located here. As was the custom, a large swan was painted on the sign that hung above the entrance. (Similarly, an eagle graced the Eagle Tavern a block away.) Jack Jouett's father was the tavernkeeper, and this was also the Jouett home. And it was here that the Virginia legislature met in 1781 after they fled from Richmond. Here also in 1812 was the War Office. By 1832 the wooden building had decayed and finally collapsed.

If you cross over to Court House Square, you'll see a large map protected by glass. This gives the layout of the village of Charlottesville in 1828. All buildings known to have existed then are shown. You can see from this map how small Charlottesville really was . . . and how far away the university and Monticello must have seemed!

When Albemarle's county seat was moved to Charlottesville in 1762, a frame building, the Court House, was erected on this site. Behind the Court House, to provide swift justice, were the jail, pillory and whipping post. The rear section of the present building replaced the original structure in 1803. The facade and front portico you see today were completed after the Civil War. The building was restored, remodeled and enlarged in 1938. Jefferson's will is displayed inside the County Clerk's Office next to the Court House.

The Court House and Court Square were the center of village activity. Church services were held here on Sundays, and, because the four prominent denominations could not afford their own churches, they rotated services. Thus every fourth Sunday the Presbyterians would take charge, to be followed the next Sunday by the Anglicans, and so on. Everyone attended, leading Jefferson to call the Court House the "Common Temple."

But Court Square was hardly a place of solemnity. Here elections were held and here free, white, male landowners came to vote and participate in raucous political celebrations. Across from the Court House were the Eagle and Swan taverns. All around were small stores and businesses. And local vendors hawked their goods from the streets. On court days hundreds of citizens flocked to town for the big event—a combination of business, reunion and good times.

In front of the Court House stands the weathered statue of a Confederate soldier, a 1909 memorial to Albemarle's volunteers. The statue is flanked by two cannons, plugged and useless now, only relics of the bitter struggle that tore the nation apart. But oldtimers remember an interesting story about these cannons. Some of the details have been blurred by time and telling but this is the way it goes.

An old man who once was a cannoneer in the Confederate Army lived not far from Court Square. On days when the weather was pleasant he would spend hours sitting on a bench near the monument. The cannons had a special meaning for him and brought back many stirring memories of battles where he had helped fire deadly rounds at the invading Yankees. The old soldier was a familiar figure to lawyers and county employees at the Court House and they often exchanged greetings with him in passing. People smiled and shook their heads when they happened to see him patting his favorite cannon or going through the motions of loading it for firing. A harmless old man engaging in fantasies.

But one Fourth of July morning, when the first pale light of dawn was spreading across the sky, the town was abruptly awakened by a tremendous blast that shook the buildings around Court Square and even broke some windows. The first people to arrive on the scene of the explosion saw the old soldier standing behind the still smoking cannon. He was leaning on his cane and seemed a little dazed from the blast but there was a vague, gleeful smile of fulfillment on his face.

The cannon was pointing down Fifth Street and wads and scraps of paper were scattered along the street for over three blocks.

After they recovered from their astonishment, the people gradually pieced together what had happened. Unknown to anyone else, the old man had cleverly placed a big charge of powder in the cannon. Then he had wadded up wet paper into balls of various sizes and rammed them into the cannon's barrel and tamped them down with his stout cane. When he had filled the cannon right up to the mouth, he waited for the appropriate time to light it off.

The scolding the old man got didn't seem to bother him at all. This was his time of glory, the brightest moment of his declining years, and he obviously enjoyed his role as a local celebrity.

The cannon still points down Fifth Street but it can no longer be fired. Never again will it rudely rouse the sleeping town to celebrate the Fourth. But it is said if you are in Court Square on a warm, sunny day and stand by the old cannons when everything is quiet, the breeze blowing softly through the trees may bring you the faint sound of gentle laughter, as if someone is chuckling over his little joke.

In the park next to the Court House is a statue of Stonewall Jackson, sculpted in 1921 by Charles Keck. Because Keck

succeeded in capturing the appearance and sensation of movement, this is generally regarded as one of the world's finest equestrian statues. Keck so wanted his statue to be accurate that he came to Albemarle to study the form of Virginia horses and style of riding equipment used by Jackson.

Spend a couple of minutes looking (really looking) at the statue and you'll feel the energy and determination Keck achieved. The noble pedestal of the Keck statue also deserves your attention. The gracefully detailed figures of Faith and Valor, supporting and leading Jackson, seem to move forward from the pedestal with power of their own. (Two blocks further west on Jefferson Street is a more conventional equestrian statue of Robert E. Lee. You'll see that the statue of Lee has the restrained formality of a slow-moving parade.)

Across the street, from 400 to 418 East Jefferson, is a row of buildings dating from 1803-1815. These brick buildings were used as residences, offices and shops. At 410 East Jefferson is the Butler-Norris House, built shortly after 1779. It is the oldest remaining original house within the "village."

Around the corner at 211 to 213 Fourth Street (NE) are several townhouses built around 1832. They are excellent examples of early nineteenth-century American architecture.

As you walk around Charlottesville, take note of the many fine houses of worship, some, such as Christ Episcopal Church (Second Street, West, at High), dating back to the 1800's. You'll see how local architecture shows the influence of Jefferson and classicism and also the "new" styles of each period. Temple Beth Israel, at 301 Jefferson, shows a startling "American Gothic" influence. (Beth Israel was originally built in 1882 and was later moved, brick by brick, by the city to its present location when the city needed the land.) Christ Episcopal owes much to the Victorian English Gothic Revival. And the First Methodist at First and Jefferson is adapted from churches by Christopher Wren.

At the Northwest corner of Second and Jefferson, at 109 East Jefferson, is a large brick home built in 1814 by Col. John R. Jones, a friend of Jefferson. Called "Social Hall," it is a fine copy of British eighteenth-century Georgian homes.

If you are especially interested in architecture, walk up Second Street two blocks from Jefferson Street past High, to 422 and 426 Second Street, East. The house at 422 was built in 1839 and the one at 426 in 1826.

From the "Social Hall" cross Jefferson Street. McIntire Library is on your left. It is named after Paul Goodloe McIntire, a local philanthropist responsible for many of the statues and civic buildings in Charlottesville.

Across from the library is Lee Park, with its statue of General Lee on his beloved horse, Traveller. The statue is by Leo Lentelli.

Lee Park makes an enjoyable place for a breather in your tour. Because it is located on a rise, you'll often feel refreshing breezes during warm summer days. And there is plenty of shade under the old trees. The park is especially lovely in spring when the Japanese flowering cherry is in bloom and the huge weeping willow is putting forth pale green tendrils that float on the wind.

Walk down First Street past Market Street to Main, where the "Downtown Mall" is an evermore successful attempt to

revitalize the downtown area. Books, clothes, trinkets—just about everything. If you enjoy shopping, you'll probably want to take advantage of this break from history.

But in Charlottesville the past is everywhere. The friendly, chatty atmosphere of today's mall recalls Charlottesville's Main Street as it was over half a century ago.

Those were the days when the Old Hardware Store, now converted into a restaurant, was in reality a hardware store, with an impressive assortment of screws, bolts, nails, tools and countless other items. These were packed close together on shelves that reached all the way to the two-story ceiling and could be reached on ladders that rolled along a track. Some of the old-fashioned atmosphere—including a ladder— has been retained in the restaurant.

But nothing remains to identify another store, an old confectionery, with a big awning that rolled down on a metal frame and created a welcome rectangle of shade on a blazing July day on Main Street. A thirsty little boy or girl could happily escape from the hot sidewalk into the cool, dim interior of the store, where the air was stirred by big wooden blades of a slow-moving ceiling fan. With great expectations,

clutching a nickel tightly, you would approach a round, marble-topped table and sit on one of the little chairs with twisted wire backs and legs. An ice cream soda? What flavor? It was real ice cream and bubbly carbonated water from a fountain faucet that could send the water squirting out violently in a tiny, sharp stream that made the soda froth up in the glass, served in a shiny metal holder. Carefully you lifted the metal top from the glass cylinder holding the paper straws and took one straw, only one, because you wanted to sip the soda slowly and make it last as long as you could. Then the ecstasy of that first sip of the sweet, cool fluid with the vanilla flavor and the peppery sting of carbonated water. And reaching in with a long-handled spoon to dig out the first cold, rich bite of vanilla ice cream. You were lost in a delicious world of taste and smell . . . a world long whirled away. A time before traffic took over the streets. There was room at the curb for everybody, even the occasional buggy mingling with the Model T's. The milk man and the ice man clip-clopped along in horse-drawn delivery wagons. (The milkman's horse knew the customers well and covered the route with only a few terse directions from the milkman who walked alongside.) And the track of the old electric trolley cars ran right down the middle of Main Street. How they whined and groaned as they struggled up Vinegar Hill, which was steeper than it is today and lined with small places of business.

Craving an ice cream soda after these musings on Main Street past? Try the Old Hardware Store (316 East Main), now converted into restaurants with a soda fountain and an arcade of shops.

At the end of the mall at Sixth and Main is the modern City Hall with its three statues of Jefferson, Madison and Monroe. If you look south, down the hill, you'll see what is now the Amtrak station, another building that shows a strong classical influence in its porticos and trim.

Return by Fifth Street to Court Square. Along the way at Market Street is a marker near the site where Monroe once lived for a year.

Back to Court Square and the lofty, humane thoughts of Jefferson, Madison and Monroe and the fine statue of Jackson.

House Tours

Throughout Charlottesville and Albemarle are many other points of interest. But many homes, estates and private clubs are not regularly open to the public. Each year during Garden Week, however, quite a few estates and homes, including professors' residences in the Pavilions on the Lawn at the university, are open for house tours.

The 1740 House

The 1740 House is located one and a half miles past the Boar's Head Inn on 250 W. Originally called the "D.S. Place" or "D.S. Tavern," it was built on an original land grant at a major crossroads. From 1785 it was operated as a tavern by Claudius Buster, and in 1810 John Marshall (Chief Justice of the Supreme Court) acquired it. The small eastern section, once the unattached kitchen, was joined at some time to the larger section, which was the tavern. The tavern section is now a private residence, but in the kitchen and central section, you'll find a delightful shop with fine antiques, many from the eighteenth century.

Statues

In addition to those described on this tour and the campus walk, two other statues are notable.

The Lewis and Clark statue, sculpted in 1919 by Charles Keck, enobles Meriwether Lewis and William Clark. But there is a third important figure—Sacajawea, their young Indian guide who is holding her baby. The statue is at Main and Ridge, near the City Market.

The George Rogers Clark statue (1922) is located in a triangle of land near Thirteenth Street on Main. Sculpted by Robert Ingersol Aitken, it shows Clark conferring with an Indian chief. Five other figures complete the dynamic grouping.

Art Galleries and Museums

The Bayly Museum — Rugby Road, one block off University
   Avenue   924-3592
   Tuesday - Sunday, 1 - 5 P.M.

The Bayly houses the permanent collection of the University of Virginia. The museum is in a stately, brick building—very regal and elegant. The collection is neither immense nor truly outstanding. Maybe this is its virtue—you are not overwhelmed by volume and magnificence. You'll see nicely displayed representative works from masters of several periods—here a Rembrandt, there a Matisse.

There's European and American sculpture, seventeenth and eighteenth century European paintings, art from Jefferson's time, nineteenth and twentieth century American paintings, plus oriental, American Indian and contemporary pieces.

One of the most unusual works is Salvador Dali's interpretation of the tranquilizer Miltown.

Charlottesville

Shows by local artists, usually members of the Albemarle Art Association, are hung regularly at Piedmont Virginia Community College (up the hill from the Bicentennial Visitors' Center), the Gordon Avenue Branch Library (1500 Gordon Ave.), the airport, City Hall and, occasionally, elsewhere. Check local papers for details.

Crafters' Gallery — 250 West (9 miles)   295-7006
   Tuesday - Sunday, 10 A.M. - 6 P.M.

Stand still and let your eyes wander around a display of pottery. Stand still and concentrate on the detail in lucite etchings. This is one gallery-shop where you have to stand still, slow down and tune into the individual pieces. Then, all of a sudden, you'll discover a perfect pot, a wonderful mobile, a fine batik . . .

Crafters' Gallery is a good outlet for talented local and non-local craftspeople. The owners are selective; the quality is high. Individual artists are also featured in changing exhibitions. And there's so much, it's almost like a crafts' show.

The mood is appropriately relaxed and hand-hewn— Crafters' Gallery is in an old barn set among rolling hills.

Pottery, lucite etchings, stained glass, weaving, tincraft, macrame, jewelry, quilts, plus lots, lots more. For the quality, most prices are quite reasonable.

McGuffey Art Center — 201 Second Street, N.W.   295-7973
   Tuesday - Saturday, 10 A.M. - 5 P.M. Sunday, 1 - 5 P.M.

On top of a hill in downtown Charlottesville is the old McGuffey elementary school, now successfully recycled as the new McGuffey Art Center.

Instead of demolishing this archetypal, big, old, red brick school, the city agreed to deed it to a group of artists. The city got it fit enough to meet the fire code, and the artists took care of renovating and sprucing it up.

About fifty artists have studios here. The low cost of studio rental leaves them free to experiment and develop without pressure to produce for sales.

102

You'll want to visit the display and sales room, of course, but allow time for wandering around from floor to floor and seeing works in progress and racks of completed projects.

The McGuffey also offers classes in arts, crafts, dance, yoga for adults and children.

Pentagram Gallery — 7 Elliewood Avenue   977-3910
    Monday - Saturday, 9 A.M. - 6 P.M.
The front half of Pentagram is a crafts shop with prisms, jewelry, sketches, carvings, etc.

Space in the small gallery in back is shared by exhibitions and a matting/framing operation.

2nd Street Gallery — 116 Second Street, N.E.   977-7284
    Tuesday - Saturday, 11 A.M. - 4 P.M.
New exhibitions each month of contemporary paintings, graphics, sculpture and photographics. Some artists are local, but 2nd Street Gallery also shows accomplished artists from all over.

Highlight of their year is the annual juried show.

The gallery is a non-profit corporation, but works shown are usually for sale.

University of Virginia
In addition to the Bayly (see above), the university has exhibitions at Alderman Library, the Health Science Library, Newcomb Hall and elsewhere. Check local papers for details.

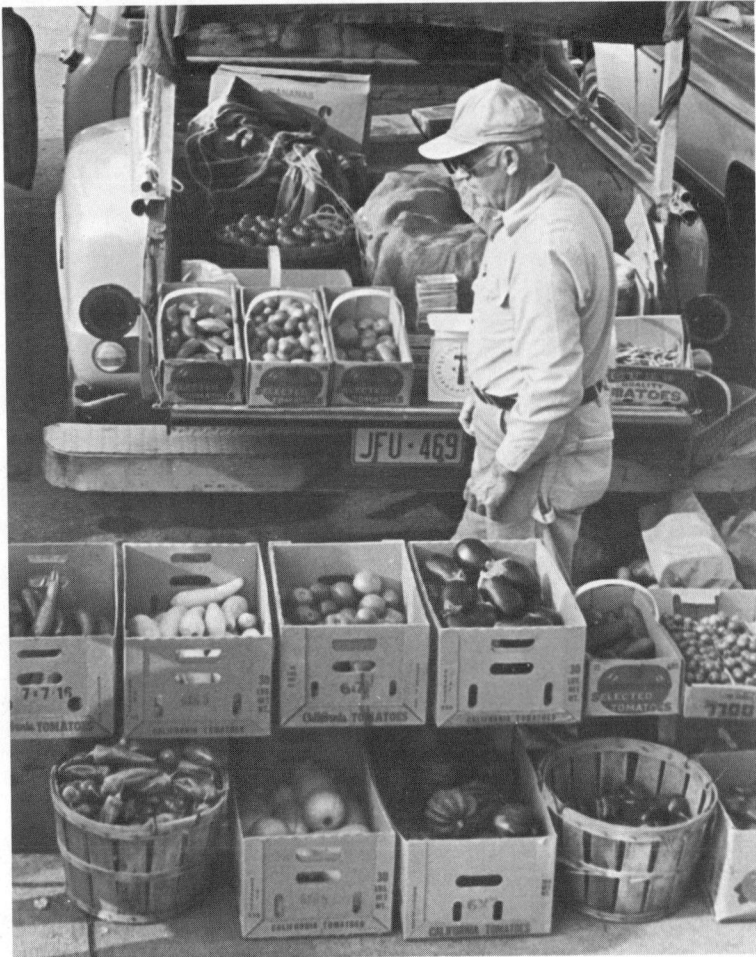

Special Activities

City Market

Tuesday, Friday and Saturday mornings, July - October. Saturday mornings in June. West Main Street at Ridge Street on hill. Crafts and local produce. How long has it been since you've tasted a dessert made with tart cherries picked *that* morning?

Crafts Fair of Virginia Crafts Council

Mid-April at University Hall. Hundreds of Virginia crafts people gather for the display and sale of their traditional and contemporary wares.

Dogwood Festival

Mid-April throughout Charlottesville. Dogwood sales, amusement rides, firework displays, track meets, fashion shows, chicken BBQ's. Etc., Etc., Etc. This is a community's spring celebration.

Fourth of July

Fireworks at McIntire Park.

Garden Week

The last full week in April. Local garden clubs organize house and garden tours of historic, beautiful Charlottesville and Albemarle homes, including magnificent country estates and UVa Pavilion homes. Private homes on the garden tour are not open at other times to the public. This is a glorious week to visit—Charlottesville is in bloom.

Garden Week is conducted by the Garden Club of Virginia and is celebrated throughout the state. But it is not just a self-serving display. Money raised by the clubs makes possible many important beautification programs in Virginia. The serpentine walls and lovely formal gardens at the university were restored and planted by the Garden Club of Virginia. And it was through their efforts that Monticello's gardens were rebuilt to look much as Jefferson planned them.

If you are interested in "House & Garden," this is the week to visit Virginia.

For dates and information, write Historic Garden Week Headquarters, 12 East Franklin Street, Richmond, Virginia 23219.

Jaycee Circus

Early May.

Jaycee Fun Fair

Mid-August. Amusement rides and carnival.

McCormick Observatory

1st and 3rd Fridays, 9-11 p.m. No charge. Star treks, weather permitting. Alternative programs in inclement weather. Go west on McCormick Road off Emmet Street.

Summer Band Concerts

Alternate Tuesdays. Usually 8 p.m. No charge. The Municipal Band of Charlottesville was organized in 1922 and has been ruffling and flourishing ever since. About 90 men and women of all ages and professions rehearse once a week throughout the year. Concerts are held on alternate Tuesday evenings in summer, usually on the Mall.

A good band playing a wide variety of compositions, cool breezes pulsing across the Mall . . . "a delightful time was had by all."

Summer Produce

The ripening of sour cherries followed by sweet raspberries, organic Georgia Belle peaches or old-fashioned Albemarle pippin apples is part of an annual ritual—the celebration of the season and the harvesting of the season's fruit. Try the city market or check the papers for farmers who sell direct from their farms. Peach or apple picking and a picnic lunch make a good outing.

Thanksgiving and Christmas—Feasts and Celebrations at the Boar's Head Inn

Participate in a Colonial Thanksgiving or a medieval Christmas complete with costumed musicians and traditional treats. At Christmas feasts you'll have wassail, yule logs, carols, jugglers, trumpeters and, yes, a boar's head, in addition to a 7-course meal. For more information write the Boar's Head Inn, Ednam Forest, P.O. Box 5185, Charlottesville, Virginia 22903.

Theater

The Charlottesville area has several active theater groups. Check Box offices or the Bicentennial Visitor Center for more information.

Blue Ridge Playhouse (Summer stock at Dyke, Va.) 985-2811
Four County Players (Barboursville) 703-832-3987

108

Heritage Repertory Company (Professional, summer)
924-3376
Shenandoah Dinner Theater (250 West) 977-5990
Virginia Players 924-3376

On-Going Activities

Lectures, concerts, recitals, dances, movies, discos, plays,
etc., etc., etc. Thanks to the University and its influence,
Charlottesville is culturally active. Check the Daily Progress
(Charlottesville), Cavalier Daily (UVa) or Charlottesville
Times (Weekly) for calendar of events.

Twenty-three Things
To Do on Weekends

1. Visit the City Market
2. Take the Charlottesville Walking Tour
3. Have brunch (C&O, Court Square Tavern, Martha's, Virginian)
4. Build a kite
5. Fly a kite
6. Feed the squirrels on campus
7. Roam through Foods of all Nations, plan a picnic
8. Take a country road
9. Have a picnic
10. Pick wildflowers
11. Go antiquing
12. Capture the season's mood in a photo or painting
13. Hike from Monticello to Ash Lawn
14. Go horseback riding
15. Visit the local galleries

110

16. Tube down a river
17. Pick fruit
18. Go skiing (Wintergreen, Bryce, Massanutten)
19. Play frisbee on the Lawn
20. Visit Scottsville and take the ferry
21. Take the University tour
22. Read the New York Times
23. Walk around campus or Court Square early in the morning

Restaurants

IN the past few years Charlottesville's restaurant scene has burgeoned with new, usually modest, often outstanding restaurants. They are generally started with lots of hopes and dreams, an inventive cook, a sense of integrity, little restaurant experience and precious little capital.

Usually the chefs are self-trained, but the influence of Julia Child and Adelle Davis is clear. These new chefs take cooking seriously, but they have fun creating the day's offerings. They steer away from meat-potato-spiced-apple cliches and from unwrap-microwave-serve kitchens. Menus change daily, the food is fresh, the meals are imaginative.

Costs are kept reasonably low, usually within a student's budget. Even credit cards are out in some places because they would add to costs. You may find plants hanging from the ceiling or antiques attached to the walls, but decor is often kept plain.

Probably because many of these small restaurants are owned by the young people who run them, a lot of pride goes into the food and service. There are occasional slips, but the quality is generally consistent.

On the whole, we have found Charlottesville's motel and chain food unimaginative and on occasion inedible. Even some breakfasts have been indigestible. Maybe the restaurant business is a tribute to local enterprise. Anyway, you'll probably have the most enjoyable meals if you dine at restaurants that are building a steady, faithful clientele.

Surely there are other good restaurants in town. These are ones we know and can recommend, some more heartily than others.

As You Like It —2119 Ivy Road   977-2714
   10 A.M.-Midnight
   Snacks and Light Meals. Also take-out.

If you like ice cream and frozen yogurt, you will like As You Like It. Choose from 30 ice creams, 6 sherbets, 5 ices and 2 frozen Dannon yogurts—plus nuts, sauces, fruits, whipped cream. The menu is a play on the Shakespearian theme and the sandwiches and ice creams make bardic allusions.

While waiting for your order, play the game, "If you were a sandwich, what sandwich would you be?" Henry VIII is, of course, a roast beef sandwich (although we thought it a bit skimpy), and King Lear has become a vegetarian mushroom and melted cheese. Hamlet took a namesake and became a ham and cheese (fortunately not Danish). But how did Richard III become a B.L.T.? And how were Romeo and Juliet transformed into good chef salads?

But, really, ice cream's the thing here. Iago's Desire, Othello's Revenge and Touchstone's Own will surely cure a lean and hungry look!

The Boar's Head Inn — Rt. 250 West   296-2181
   8-10:30 A.M., Noon-2 P.M., 6-9 P.M.
   Beer, Wine and Cocktails. Lighter meals continuously in lounge, "Downstairs." Entertainment. Coats required at dinner and ties preferred.

The Boar's Head Inn finally seems to have its kitchen under control. We were disappointed the first few times we ate here, so it was not with great expectations that we returned. We were happily surprised.

114

The candlelit room is itself very pretty—dark rough-hewn beams and wainscoting, set off by the Wedgwood blue and cream decor. We had always wanted the food to be as good as the room was pretty. And this time it was. The duck was young and fresh (not frozen, but also, we were assured, not from the Boar's Head pond) and not fatty. The prime rib was large, tender and nicely cooked. Fresh greens and spoonbread were fine. The house wine was decent enough and the fresh watercress salad was superb. Cellophane wrapped crackers seemed tackily out of place, but we weren't expecting perfection.

Lunch is lighter—sandwiches, salads and daily special entrees, stews and the like.

For breakfast you have your choice of a large buffet (good biscuits and muffins) or a complete breakfast menu. Even this buffet was well above average.

"Downstairs" is the cocktail lounge where you can have more casual, buffet-style meals. Different cuisines are currently served on different nights of the week. "If this is chow mein, it must be Tuesday?"

C&O Restaurant — 515 East Water Street   296-8280

Lunch—11:30 A.M.-3 P.M., Mon.-Sat.
Brunch—Sunday, 11 A.M.-2 P.M.
Dinner—Two seatings at 6:30 and 9 P.M.
Closed during August.
Beer, Wine, Cocktails. Light meals, lunch, cocktails served downstairs. Tables outdoors in season. Jackets are appropriate for men. Reservations for dinner and Sunday brunch.

If Jefferson were alive today, the C&O would be his favorite Charlottesville restaurant. High praise that, for Jefferson, you may remember, was inordinately fond of good, imaginative French cooking. He would be delighted with the C&O's very good, very imaginative dinners.

Perhaps, like all artists, the C&O's chef has off nights. Each time we eat here it is with the fear that they can never again match the last performance. We are put at ease when at one bite all taste buds seem to explode. Ah! A masterful play on the palate. An exhilarating experience. The C&O is the only restaurant we know that continually pushes each dish beyond the diner's expectations.

Don't be put off by the appearance. From the outside the C&O does look like a greasy spoon cafe. It takes its name from an earlier and less illustrious restaurant that once occupied the same building. The name referred to the Chesapeake and Ohio railroad depot (now AMTRAK) across the street. Anyway, today's C&O is a pearl.

The restaurant is upstairs, the bar on the ground floor. The dining room's decor is very plain—all ivory, including the floor. White plates, white linens, antique silverplate and fresh flowers. All understated and pleasant. The C&O has fewer than a dozen tables, but there is never a rushed feeling as there are only two well-spaced seatings each night. Dinner is a long, indulgent affair—plan at least two hours.

The service totters between being impeccable and overly mannered, but it is in the best country-French style. The average height of the waiters in 1976-77 is even of interest. They probably set a record for being the tallest team of waiters in the world.

The menu changes daily. You'll always have your choice of about five first courses and about five entrees. Be sure to have your waiter describe each dish because the chef takes wonderful liberties with what may sound ordinary.

First will come a thin loaf of French bread and fine, unsalted butter.

Be sure to have a first course. The truffled pate is delicious, but filling. The soups are lighter and always unusual.

For main courses you'll probably have a choice of the day's quiche (superb crust), steak, fish (the stuffed fresh trout is a winner), a veal dish (perhaps stuffed with Boursin and herbs, sauteed, and glazed with a thin wine sauce), perhaps a game dish (rabbit with fruit) and, if you are very, very lucky, stuffed Cornish game hen.

Imagine a Cornish game hen with a giblet forcemeat (Thanksgiving stuffing was never like this!) served on top of a buttered canape spread with pate. Unimaginably sublime.

116

Yes, and even the vegetables get words of praise. Just almost underdone and wonderfully seasoned. Maybe a squash-onion-tomato combination, or garlicky green beans, or fresh broccoli with a divine Hollandaise.

And after all that comes a refreshing French salad. Crisp Boston lettuce lightly coated with a classic dressing. Very simple. Very good.

And then do be sure to have dessert. Sundaes and parfaits are always available. Skip them. Indulge in the C&O's dessert fantasies. Perhaps they'll have Grand Marnier pie—so delicate it could take flight. Or the Charlotte Russe that makes Sara Lee look like a country bumpkin. Or the Dobos Torte, made just as it should be with real butter cream and a beautiful caramel glaze. Yes, do have dessert.

The C&O has a good wine list, and their house wines are

reasonable and delightful. Mixed drinks are well made. The coffee could improve.

The downstairs bar is dark and rustic, a perfect place for lunch or an aperitif before going upstairs. Lunches are much simpler—pates, salads, quiches. Brunches are inventive—brioche or croissant, a good fruit compote, omelets, trout, mixed grill and the like. And of course, dessert, by all means.

Expensive? For Charlottesville, yes, although other restaurants are as much. In a large city you would expect to pay much more for disappointingly average French food. But at the C&O you will not be disappointed. Unlike so many other restaurants, you will feel satisfied, maybe even exhilarated, by a worthy performance.

Christian's Deli — McIntire Plaza   293-3000
11 A.M.-9 P.M., Mon.-Thurs. 11 A.M.-10 P.M., Fri.-Sat.
Closed Sunday.
Beer and Wine. Also take-out and delivery. Parties catered.

"For this he spent four years in college," is the motto of this delicatessen popular with UVa students and faculty. Unemployed Ph.D.'s would suggest he could have done worse.

You'll find the usual infinite range of deli sandwiches, plus spicy submarines, chili and daily specials—soups, omelets and the like.

As this book goes to press, Christian's is planning to open a new branch opposite Best Products at the Albemarle Shopping Center.

Corner Delicatessen — 9 Elliewood Ave.   977-6677
10:30 A.M.-10 P.M., Mon.-Thurs. 10:30 A.M.-Midnight, Fri.-Sat.
11:30 A.M.-9 P.M., Sun.
Beer. Entertainment on Weekends. Also take-out and catering.

Tucked away in an Elliewood English basement is the Corner Deli—a perfect place for lunch after a campus tour or for a snack after several hours at the library. The owners take pride in preparing and serving good sandwiches, and the prices are reasonable.

118

Possible sandwich combinations are practically infinite—
20 or so main ingredients, 9 different breads and 16 or so
garnishes. Concoct a Virginia ham and turkey (homecooked!)
with slaw (homemade!) and provolone on pumpernickel. Or
maybe a roast beef with sliced N.Y. olives and mayo. Or a
more traditional shrimp or egg salad. Fresh soups and good
cheesecake. Imported and domestic beers.

The atmosphere is gentle, casual, comfortable and relaxed.
After you order and pick up your sandwiches, you might settle
back to watch an old movie on the TV or take lunch outdoors
to the back courtyard.

The Corner Deli could quickly become an old friend.

Court Square Tavern — Court Square   296-6111
    9 A.M.-2 A.M., Mon.-Fri. 11 A.M.-2 A.M., Sat.-Sun.
    Beer, Wine and Cocktails.

In the old days you might have seen Thomas Jefferson,
James Monroe and James Madison walking around the Court
Square. And if the Court Square Tavern had existed then, you
could conceivably have joined the Big Three for a stout or
sherry in their local tavern. Alas. Conversations are still
occasionally spirited if not of earth-molding significance.

Court Square Tavern doesn't copy the superficialities of the
typical British pub with its dart board, pub mugs and dusty
memorabilia. But it does achieve the feeling of certain
neighborhood pubs. Enjoyable people, tasteful surroundings,
interesting conversations and, yes, good food. It's a comfortable place to talk and talk and talk.

Meals are mostly sandwiches, soups and salads, plus daily specials, lamb stew, roast beef and the like. Sunday's brunch includes Virginia ham, eggs, fried chicken.

In addition to good sherries and Guiness, the Court Square makes a superb, and unusual, Bloody Mary.

The Fish House — 20 Elliewood Ave.   295-8537
    5-11 P.M.

    Beer, Wine and Cocktails.

French-fried onion fans will be in heaven here. The crust is light and flaky, and the onions still have a bit of crispness.

The seafood gets the same delicate treatment. Everything on the seafood platter—oysters, scallops, shrimp and sea perch—is fresh-tasting and very lightly breaded and fried.

The menu changes often, depending on what is fresh and available. We have also enjoyed the fresh trout and the oysters casino.

In warm weather the Fish House opens up a pleasant patio with a brick floor and some hanging plants here and there. Wild honeysuckle in the spring lends an enchanting, outside-of-the-city atmosphere. In winter a fire is lit in the fireplace where the bar is cozy and the drinks are fresh and well mixed.

Very enjoyable.

Gaslight Fountain Restaurant —
               Barracks Road Shopping Center   295-8067

    Lunch—Noon-2 P.M., Mon.-Sat.

    Dinner—5:30-10 P.M., Mon.-Thurs.

             5:30-11 P.M., Fri.-Sat.

             5:30-11 P.M., Sun. (Fall to Spring).

    Beer, Wine, Cocktails. Piano, Mon.-Sat., 7-10 P.M.

Shad roe. Shad roe. Shad roe. Even though its been frozen, it's awfully good. And where else can you order it in, say, September?

The Gaslight seems especially popular at lunchtime. It's a mixed crowd—businessmen who are obviously regulars, clutches of ladies meeting for sociable little luncheons, and stragglers in from the shopping center.

Lunches steer away from beef—eggs, fish, veal, chicken and salads are more likely than hamburgers. Duck and lobster are dinner favorites.

But some of us never stray from Shad Roe.

Hardware Store Restaurants —
316 East Main Street   977-1518

Closed Sun.
Soda Fountain Restaurant 11:30 A.M.-10 P.M.
The Offices 11:30 A.M.-2:30 P.M., 6-10 P.M.
The Loft (Lounge) 8:30 P.M.-1 A.M.
Entertainment some evenings in lounge. Also take-out.

In this emporium of foods, there's something for everyone—from take-out ice cream, Blum pretzels, Godiva chocolates, bake shop sweets to hot dogs turning on a grill to a crepe bar to a casual soda fountain restaurant to a more leisurely dining spot to a cocktail lounge.

The Hardware Store Soda Fountain Restaurant is the more casual of the two dining rooms. You can sit in booths on the main floor or at tables on the mezzanine. The menu is huge—full meals and short order snacks—but the quality has varied. Last time we ate there it was pretty good. Ice cream parlor specials—sundaes, sodas and the like—are always favorites. It's fun to watch them being concocted and to see whipped cream flow from a pastry bag instead of a pressurized can. Slides of Charlottesville and the area are projected onto overhead screens. Altogether an entertaining place.

The Offices is a small restaurant in the back. It's darker and quieter. Here fine, courteous service encourages you to enjoy a relaxed meal. Choose the daily special, perhaps a seafood

121

casserole, or have good soup or a huge salad.

Upstairs in back is the Loft, the cocktail lounge.

The Hickory Chip — Eleventh and Main   296-8715
11 A.M.-2 P.M.
Take-out.

The pit's out back. That's wood smoke in the air. Ah, Barbeque! For a fast meal when you crave barbeque, this is the place. Sliced or chopped, beef or pork, sandwiches or platters. Chicken, ribs, hamburgers, hot dogs. Everything is smoked or grilled here—sandwiches and shakes are made to order.

The great BBQ War will probably always divide the South. In the heart of Virginia, the Hickory Chip takes sides with "North Carolina Style"—the sauce is thinner, sourer, pepperier and always accompanied by cole slaw. (Why cole slaw? Who knows, but you get used to it, and after a while they seem quite natural together.) South of Carolina and west of Virginia the sauce is thicker, redder, sweeter, smokier, spicier.

Those of us raised on *real* barbeque will never really get used to the Carolina style. However, for barbeque in Virginia, the Hickory Chip's BBQ is pretty good stuff. (It satisfies the craving but whets the deep, deep hunger.) To a native Virginian, this is good barbeque.

Hollymead Inn — Rt. 29 North (several miles)   973-8488
11:30 A.M.-2 P.M., 5-9:30 P.M., Tues.-Sat.
Beer, Wine and Cocktails. Cocktail Lounge.
Reservations advised.

The Hollymead Inn will take you back a couple of centuries to a house of the late 18th century. The Hessian Room, the inn's most rustic dining room, was actually built by Hessian soldiers taken prisoner during the Revolutionary War. The Wedgwood Room dates back to 1810-1820 and was once used as a private boys' school. During the restoration in 1937 another wing was added and this now includes a dining room and a small, homey, hunt-country lounge.

Downstairs is a first-rate butcher shop, the Hook & Cleaver, that supplies freshly cut meat for the restaurant. And it is the simple cuts and plainly prepared dishes that are your best bet here. By night try the delicate, moist pork chops or prime rib and by day the good, thick hamburger.

Dinners include relish trays, cinnamon rolls, salad, potato and vegetable. Desserts are very sweet and seasonal—maybe fresh strawberry shortcake or rhubarb pie.

Reservations are a must, dressing up is not, although ties and coats seem prevalent.

Japanese Steak House and Ah, So Lounge
Four Seasons Drive   973-8080
5:30-10 P.M., Sun.-Thurs. 5-10:30 P.M., Fri.-Sat.
Beer, Wine and Cocktails. Cocktail Lounge with
Entertainment 4:30 P.M.-1 A.M.

The appetizers are so good, we once had dinner in the Ah, So Lounge by nibbling our way through every appetizer on the menu. Tempuras are the specialty and they are made to order in a corner of the lounge. Choose seafood, chicken or vegetable. We are especially fond of Yaki Mandu, a rolled, fried, garlicky beef tenderloin appetizer that is light years beyond the usual egg roll. Chairs and tables are low and loungy, and the cocktail piano is nostalgic. Ah, so.

In the restaurant you have your choice of sitting at tables of regular height or of sitting on mats and dangling your feet under a sunken table. Not very oriental, perhaps, but it does create atmosphere. Eight people are usually seated together... which makes this a great place for eight friends but not for a tête à tête.

Except for tempuras, dinners are cooked on the very hot metal grill that forms your table. The fun, of course, is in watching a pretty Japanese girl in a lovely kimona toss and grill sliced meats and vegetables for your sukiyaki or teriyaki. The beef is very tender and the vegetables are still slightly crisp.

All in all, pretty good. A nice place to come with friends.

Kim's Yogurt Factory —

Fourteenth and Main (in the Mini-Mall)   296-4575
11 A.M.-Midnight

Kim's Yogurt Factory claims to have Charlottesville's finest frozen yogurt. To which we said, "Ho Hum, Dannon is Dannon." But no, somehow Kim's Danny *does* taste fresher and better. It has a wonderful, smooth flavor without the twang of some frozen yogurts. Hooray!

The menu is pretty simple. Several flavors of Dannon and Frogurt frozen yogurts and, also, ice cream. Plus several tops and bottoms—nuts, bananas, fruits, fudge, pound cake, apple pie, melon, avocado, plus a couple of salads. Plus yogurt or ice cream shakes. Plus several varieties of hot dogs. Plus Kim's special hangover remedy.

As far as we know, this is the only place in Charlottesville where orange juice is squeezed to order and where real old-fashioned lemonade is made with (gasp!) real lemons.

124

La Hacienda — 400 Emmet   295-0258
7 A.M.-11 P.M.
Beer.

This is about as American as Mexican-American food can get—it is also quite inexpensive, fast and popular.

La Hacienda opens early for breakfast. In addition to the usual, they offer a couple of border breakfasts—cheese, chili, tomato, sausage omelets and buttered flour tortillas.

For lunch and dinner—all possible combinations of tacos, tostados, enchiladas, burritos, tamales. Plus guacamole, beans, rice. Plus hot sauce. Plus Mexican beer.

La Hacienda's cheese crisp is a kind of Texican pizza—a flat flour tortilla topped with cheese plus sausage, beef or chilis. It is often served as a tasty appetizer to which you can masochistically add a fiery chili sauce.

Martha's Cafe — Elliewood Avenue   295-3418
11:30 A.M.-2 P.M., Mon.-Fri. 11:30 A.M.-2:30 or 3 P.M., Sun.
5:30-8 P.M., Mon.-Sat.

A small plaque on the fireplace mantle proclaims Martha the "Muffin Queen." Rightly so. Martha's muffins are light, delicate and not overly sweet. . . and they accompany each entree.

The menu is chalked daily on blackboards. The healthy staples are huge salads (good greens, cheese and lots of crunchy vegetables), omelets, quiches (excellent crust), a daily soup and an old-fashioned dessert. (Cherry or blueberry crunch could be your reward for having *just* a giant salad.) Coffee is rich and good.

Weekend brunches are mostly egg and cheese dishes, omelets and quiches, fresh fruits and wonderful homemade pastries. Dinners include one or two heartier entrees, a chicken marengo with wild rice or a vegetable curry.

Martha's is in an old house on Elliewood near the university. Meals are served in two rooms of the house and in warm weather in the small courtyard in front. Plan on arriving early—sometimes there's a line.

Informal, comfortable, reasonable, friendly. It's all very good, and sometimes inspired.

Monticello Room — Court Square   296-6111
    Luncheon - Noon-2 P.M., Mon.-Fri.
    Seafood Buffet - 6-9 P.M., Fri.-Sat.
    Sunday Dinner - Noon-5:30 P.M.
    Beer, Wine and Cocktails. (Court Square Tavern Lounge and Restaurant downstairs.)

"Well, yes, thank you, maybe just one or two more oysters. . . Newburg?. . . Well, just a smidgen. And what a beautiful flounder. . . maybe just a little of that. But I think I'll pass up the roast beef, for now at least."

Friday and Saturday night at the Monticello's seafood buffet. There's *so* much to choose from and it's all *so* good. From raw clams and oysters to delicate fried oysters to a creamy sauced this and a spicy sauced that, through more than half a dozen rich seafood offerings to a huge steamship round of beef. Plus salads, vegetables, spoonbread. You'll be tempted to have "just a taste" of everything.

The Monticello Hotel was opened in 1926 and has now been converted into private residences. The dining room was obviously modeled after Jefferson's home. The chairs, for example, are replicas of those in Jefferson's dining room, and the high ceilings, crown molding and wainscoting, candles and floral arrangements give a Jeffersonian elegance to the room. It's the sort of hotel dining room where people used to go for Sunday dinner, and that custom is still intact today at the Monticello.

This is also a good place for a quiet lunch overlooking Court Square. Reasonable prices, ample portions and a daily menu that might include avocado stuffed with crab salad, chicken livers on rice, broiled fresh fish, crab cakes and a fruit-salad plate.

If you are planning to go to the Seafood Buffet, have a light lunch.

126

The Mousetrap and Omelette Room
100 14th Street   29-MOUSE
Mousetrap — 11 A.M.-12:30 A.M., 7 Days.
Omelette Room — 6 P.M.-Midnight, Thurs.-Sat.
11 A.M.-2 P.M., Sun.
Beer and Wine. Entertainment.

When you enter the Mousetrap you are given a ticket. Everything you eat or drink, plus "obligatory gratuities," will be recorded on your ticket. This clever system allows people to move from room to room and to mix.

Downstairs is the Mousetrap where the favorites are char-broiled hamburgers (mouse) and cheeseburgers (rat) and salads. Beer is on tap and flows freely from 3 - 6 P.M. during the Mousetrap's popular "Get Together Hours."

The Old Virginia decor is carried throughout the Mouse-trap's several rooms. Beer is served in Mason jars and horse and barn artifacts decorate the walls.

Upstairs is the Omelette Room and a more intimate atmosphere. You'll find all sorts of crepes and omelets, including fancy dessert versions. The wine list is touted as one of the largest in the state. This is a good place to come for a light meal and long conversation after a movie or concert.

The Ordinary at Michie Tavern —
Rt. 53 (Road to Monticello)   977-1234
Buffet Lunch. 11:15 A.M.-3:30 P.M.
Beer.

Lunch at the Ordinary at Michie Tavern is designed to give you the experience of eating a typical colonial meal in a typical colonial setting. You'll eat in chinked log rooms with low, beamed ceilings, much like the dining room in the Michie Tavern Museum. The Ordinary was converted from a log cabin originally used over 200 years ago as slave quarters.

The "Bill of Fare" is fairly authentic. Black-eyed peas, stewed tomatoes, curd (cottage) cheese, green bean salad, cole slaw, potato salad, biscuits, fried chicken and apple cobbler. Margarine and instant tea are unfortunate modern intrusions.

The food at the Ordinary is good enough, not extraordinary.

But if you are planning a full day of sightseeing, Michie's makes a perfect lunch stop, and the Museum is certainly worthwhile. Lunch lines are often long, so plan to arrive early.

Peking Tea House — Rt. 250 West (2 miles.) 296-3023
5-11 P.M., Mon.-Sat. Noon-11 P.M., Sun.
Also take-out.

Every time we come here we want to try new dishes, but some of our favorites are irresistible.

Seldom can we turn down the Moo Shu Pork, quickly sauteed shredded vegetables and pork served with the Chinese version of crepes. You roll or fold your own—inevitably messy and inevitably good.

Fung Wong Gai would be at home on a Virginia plantation. Boned chicken stuffed with ham, lobster and vegetables, then breaded and fried.

Their Almond Gai Ding (chicken with vegetables, toasted almonds, and a hint of garlic) and Char Shu Ding (pork and vegetables) are both good. Four Seasons (lobster, duck, chicken and pork) is a crowd pleaser; it comes sizzling to the table. Some other dishes are Szechwan style—they are hotter and sourer, often with black beans and pickled vegetables.

The Peking Tea House has a fairly long menu with all the basic Chinese-American chows and chops and sweets and sours and dinners for 3, 4, 5, etc. But we find the more inventive dishes much more of a treat.

Peking Tea House appetizers are enjoyable. The Peking Platter will give you a taste of most of them.

Hot and sour soup is just that—peppery and puckery. We like it, but it does taste unusual. More popular is the 12-ingredient soup, chicken stock with a dozen goodies—mushrooms, pork, onion, etc., etc. A large pot is brought to your table and easily serves four.

Portions are reasonably priced and large. And there's not much atmosphere—in keeping with the popular theory that good Chinese restaurants should be inexpensive, serve large portions and make no attempts at decor. Peking Tea House fits these requirements and more. The rice is light and properly cooked. The tea is good, and the pot is refilled often. You'll hear chopping sounds coming from the kitchen, and your vegetables will still be slightly crisp. They are also as fresh as possible—during the summer, there's a neatly tended garden on both sides of the restaurant.

The Peking Tea House is not the best Chinese or Szechwan restaurant we have eaten at, but when we crave Chinese food, we keep coming back. And, if you are just graduating from chop suey and chow mein, venture out and try Moo Shu Pork or Almond Gai Ding or Fung Wong Gai.

Sarge's Pancake House and Restaurant —
1140 Emmet   295-0404
7 A.M.-9 P.M., Tues.-Sat. 7 A.M.-3 P.M. Sun.
Closed Mon.
Beer.

Once upon a time there were lots of restaurants like Sarge's—dependable, reasonable, short-order places you could count on for a solid breakfast or a quick snack or meal. Nothing special—always dependable. These were the places we came to after Jr. High games and dances—where we giggled and blushed and surreptiously put salt in the sugar and sugar in the salt while humiliated chaperons sat twenty feet away and tried to look oblivious.

Few of these restaurants have survived in the era of franchised, portioned, packaged, fast foods. Fortunately, Sarge's is still around. And so is the juke-box.

This is the best breakfast place we have found in Charlottesville. Good eggs (cooked as you request them), good country ham, good country sausage, good strong coffee. . . even skim milk. Pancakes, waffles and all the American breakfast staples.

For lunch or dinner we would stick to basics—hamburger steak sandwiches with onions, hoagies, french fries, fried egg and ham sandwiches. And if you want to sit and talk and talk, there's no rush.

There's no atmosphere, unless you get nostalgic about barnlike short-order restaurants of the 50's, but the service and food are just fine. The rooftop motto says that Sarge's is where town and gown and tourists meet. For good reason.

Schnitzelhouse — 2208 Fontaine Avenue   293-7185
     5:30-9:30 P.M., Tues.-Sat.
     Beer, Wine and Cocktails.

Wursts and schnitzels are specialities here and you'll have quite a variety to choose from. German sausage lovers can have bratwurst, weisswurst or knockwurst. And veal cutlet fans will find the Schnitzelhouse schnitzels a hearty change from thin French and Italian versions. Sometimes the veal is "home-grown," but always it is thick and tender. Choose your schnitzel plain, breaded, stuffed with ham and cheese, topped with an egg or sauced with mushrooms and vegetables. Entrees are served with red cabbage, spaetzle (German noodles) or potato salad.

The German theme is carried throughout. Waitresses wear colorful dirndls. Ornately decorated beer steins are displayed in a handsome case. Placemats give mini-lessons in German history. And a few German beers and wines are available.

Tortilla Flat — 16 Elliewood Avenue   977-4199
     11:30 A.M.-2:30 P.M., 7 Days
     5:30-10:30 P.M., Sun.-Thurs.
     5:30-11 P.M., Fri.-Sat.
     Beer, Wine and Cocktails.

Tortilla Flat makes a pleasant change from bordertown Mexicana. You'll find no sombreros, no marachis, no bullfighters on black velvet. The music is more likely to be classical or popular. Walls are decorated with rustic Virginiana—farm and tobacco barn antiques. Books in bookcases, plants at the window, beamed ceilings. And, in winter, a cracking fire in the stone fireplace.

Tortilla Flat is quiet, dark and comfortable. And they serve good, basic Tex-Mex food—tostados, tacos, enchiladas, chili rellenos. Try the nachos as a snack or first course with Mexican beer or a banana daiquiri.

Portions are large. A single a la carte order is sufficient for lunch or a light meal. Combination plates make substantial meals, reasonably priced. The combination enchilada plate, for example, has three well stuffed enchiladas (the cheese enchilada is a cross between butter and sunshine), rice, beans and salad. For dessert, try flan.

The most Mexican thing about Tortilla Flat is the service—mañana. Perhaps it will become more rápido. Meanwhile, relax and enjoy a leisurely meal.

University Cafeteria — 1517 West Main   295-9251
11:30 A.M.-2 P.M., Mon.-Fri. 11:30 A.M.-2:15 P.M., Sun.
4:45-8 P.M., Sun.-Fri.
Closed Sat.

If you like cafeterias, you'll surely like the University Cafeteria. It's a longtime favorite with UVa and townspeople. There's often a line, but, all in all, it's fast, reasonable and convenient.

Expect to find beef, ham, fried chicken, fish and a couple of other entrees, plus jellied, vegetable and fruit salads, assorted vegetables, fresh muffins and sweet and gooey pies and cakes.

The Virginian Inn — 1521 West Main   293-2606
11 A.M.-2 A.M.
Beer, Wine and Cocktails.

The Virginian is an archetypal college bar. It's always dark when you enter and you feel your eyes slowly adjusting to this protective inner sanctum. Cool and dark in summer, warm and dark in winter, always comfortable. How many theses and love affairs have found inspiration and sustenance in the Virginian's booths?

The Virginian is built long and narrow like a trolley, the tall wooden booths are along one side, opposite the bar and grill. Fresh flowers, blackboards chalked with daily specials, mirrors on the walls, fans on the ceilings.

The moods change by the hour and the season. On Saturdays in winter you can sit at the bar, watch football on TV and drink beer. On Sundays, bring the Times (your eyes *do* adjust) and have a Bloody Mary and eggs benedict. Weeknights, come in late for a cheese and fruit board with wine and long, serious talk. On a cold afternoon, fortify yourself with hot cider, eggnog or a good sherry.

Or make it to the Virginian any old time for lunch or dinner. The food is good and varied and fresh. From hamburgers to cheese boards to full meals. Daily specials are often a bargain—roast lamb, fresh bluefish, chicken parmesan, etc. Portions are large. Pies are homemade and imaginative—we once had a hot "spirited" apple pie with fresh, unpeeled apples and one other time an Irish coffee St. Patrick's pie.

The Virginian is part of the UVa tradition. We suspect that generations of alums return as nostalgically to the Virginian as to the Lawn and colonnades.

Food Stores

In addition to full-service restaurants that provide take-out service, there are several extraordinary food stores where you can also get provisions.

Foods of all Nations in the 7 Day Shopping Center at 2121 Ivy Road (250 W) is a Charlottesville institution. The New York Times once called it an "asset to any community," and it is a wonderful place to browse through. Anyone who enjoys cooking should make a pilgrimage here—rices, spices, mustards, teas, caviars (refrigerated, not preserved), pheasants (with feathers), regular everyday foods plus breads, beers, ports and a deli.

Carriage Food House at Rt. 29 N and Barracks Road also carries culinary exotica, but the selection is smaller. Bakery goods (maybe a loaf of French bread shaped like an alligator), freshly made sausages, baskets, unusual canned goods, beers and wines.

Blue Mountain Trading Co., 801 W. Main, is the largest health food store in town, and it is a very good one. Flours, grains, seeds, nuts, herbs. Cheese and other dairy products. Organic, fresh vegetables.

The Cellar Master at 7 Elliewood sells cheese and wine. The store is cleverly designed to resemble a wine cellar.

ABC Stores

In Virginia some groceries (most in fact) are licensed by the state to sell beer and wine. State-operated stores sell wine and harder liquors. These stores are located at 2130 Barracks Road, 200 Water St., 853 W. Main and Albemarle Square (Rt. 29 N.).

134

Shopping

Visitors to Charlottesville and Albemarle will easily find souvenirs of their trip. So many specialty shops abound that it may be easier to find the perfect, unusual, exotic gift than an ordinary hohum doodad.

There's something for everyone—from inexpensive mementos to priceless treasures, assembly line or handcrafted, brand new or eighteenth century. Even in clothing styles there is a respect for the classics—tweedy clothes that never wear out and never go out of style.

Shops are scattered all over town, but there are four main shopping areas. Downtown—the Mall plus sidestreets and parallel streets. University area—"the Corner" across from

135

UVa on University and Main Street, Elliewood Avenue, Fourteenth Street's Mini-Mall and along Main Street to about Ninth. Rt. 29 North—Emmet or 29-North, including Charlottesville's two largest shopping centers, called Barracks Road and Albemarle Square. Rt. 250 West—scattered shops off and on for miles.

Rather than recommend or describe stores, we have listed some items you can find here.

Antiques. So many. From 18th century to primitives to reproductions. Try downtown, Main Street and out 250 West.

Baskets. Clover Lawn Basket Shop (imported) on 250 West, roadside stands (native split oak) also on 250 West. And at import shops.

Caviar. Beluga, without preservatives. Foods of All Nations and Carriage House.

Dehydrated Foods for Campers. Blue Ridge Mountain Sports, 29 North.

Estates. Check classified and local realtors.

Film. Best Products (Albemarle Square), Camera Center (W. Main), Gary's Camera Shop (Barracks Road Shopping Center).

Godiva Chocolates. Hardware Store in Downtown Mall.

Headbands. Pappagallo on 250 West.

Ironwork. Custom-made, ornamental wrought iron. Harry A. Wright and Associates Steel Products.

Jeffersonia. Monticello Gift Shop and all over town.

Kites. Arnette's at "The Corner."

Lead Crystal Prisms. Pentagram on Elliewood.

Mr. Hank Originals. Women's clothes made in Charlottesville, available at Mr. Hank Boutique on Main.

Newspapers. Mincer's Pipe Shop at "The Corner."

Organic Makeup. Hardware Store in Downtown Mall and The Phoenix in Fourteenth Street Mini-Mall.

Pot Pourri. "The Original," still made in Charlottesville. Available in gift shops all over town.

Quilts. Paula Lewis near Court Square on Jefferson.

Ropes. Handmade for jumping. Bicentennial Visitor's Center.

Soaps. Meadowbrook Pharmacy on Barracks Road stocks hundreds.

Trivets. Brown's Gifts and Stedman House, both downtown, and The Very Thing at Boar's Head.

Unicycles. Schwinn Bike Shop on Preston.

Vegetables and Fruits. City Market, Ridge and Main.

Wooden Clogs. Trolls of Norway, downtown.

Xylophones. Shenanigans Toys on 250 West.

Yarns and Needlepoint Canvasses. Chimney Corner Needlework in Barracks Center.

Zinc. Blue Mountain Trading Co. and Sylvania Organic Foods, both on Main.

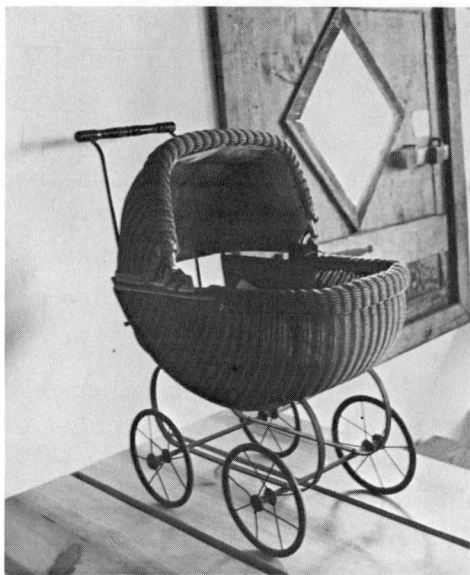

Accommodations

CHARLOTTESVILLE has an abundance of motels and yet on weekends and during the summer NO VACANCY signs line the highway. Rates also go up on big weekends and during the summer. It is best to plan ahead and make reservations. But if you do arrive without reservations and have trouble finding a motel, the Bicentennial Information Center off I-64 (Monticello exit) will help you find a room.

Several types of lodging are available.

The Boar's Head Inn is Charlottesville's only hotel-resort. It's set a couple of miles west of town in a ring of small lakes, stocked with trout and beautiful Canadian geese. Sports, shops, suites and fireplaces, a lounge and a restaurant. The rooms are tastefully decorated with colonial reproductions, nice lamps, pretty comforters, comfortable chairs. At night the cover is turned down for you. The atmosphere is not stuffy, however. You are given the homelike feeling of staying in a friend's guestroom. The Boar's Head Inn is somewhat more expensive, but it offers more, too. Make reservations well in advance for weekends.

Chain motels are carbons of their brothers and sisters elsewhere. Most are large and fairly new. Prices are generally higher than at the smaller, older local motels.

Locally owned motels have smaller rooms and are less flashy, but almost all have the necessary amenities—color TV, swimming pool, phones. Some, e.g., the Cardinal, have coin-operated vibrating beds and picnic-playground areas. These motels are somewhat older and somewhat cheaper than the chains.

Farther out of town are still smaller motels, considerably cheaper but usually without color TV, pools and phones.

If you prefer the privacy and extra space of a furnished apartment or guest house, contact Guesthouses Reservation Services. Rates vary according to the size of the apartment or house, but they are especially reasonable for a week's stay. Linens and cooking utensils are provided.

Several campgrounds are also with fifteen miles of Charlottesville.

Motels and Hotels

Boar's Head Inn	Rt. 250 W	296-2181
Cardinal Motel	Rt. 29 N	293-6188
Cavalier Inn (Best Western)	Rt. 29 N	296-8111
Econo Lodge	400 Emmet (29 N)	296-2104
Greenwood Motel	Rt. 250 W (10 mi. W)	823-8263
Holiday Inn (North)	Rt. 29 N.	293-9111
Holiday Inn (South)	I-64 & 5th	977-5100
Howard Johnson's	1309 W. Main	296-8121
Ivy Motor Court	Rt. 250 W (5 mi.)	293-3096
Jefferson Motor Lodge	Rt. 29 S (2 mi.)	296-7196
Mt. Vernon Quality Inn	Rt. 29 N	296-5501
Overlook Motel	Rt. 250 E	293-9154
Ramada Inn	1901 Emmet (29 N)	977-7700
Sheraton Inn	Rt. 250 E and I-64	977-3300
Town & Country Motor Lodge	Rt. 250 E	293-6191
Tuckahoe Motel	Rt. 250 W (15 mi.)	703-456-2161
University Lodge Motel	Rt. 29 N	293-5141
White House Motel	Rt. 250 E	296-7106

Guesthouses

Guesthouses Reservations
   Services   147 Georgetown Green   973-7403

Campgrounds

Charlottesville KOA Campgrounds	Rt. 708	296-9881
Lake Reynovia (Avon)	Rt. 742 S. (2 mi.)	296-1910
Montfair Family Resort (Crozet)	Rt. 810	822-5202
Monticello Skyline Safari Campground (Greenwood)	Rt. 250 W	703-456-6409

Other Places to Visit
in Virginia

AFTER your stay in Charlottesville and Albemarle, you may wish to visit other places of interest in Virginia. There are many. Some are listed here with brief descriptions. More detailed information may be obtained from the Western Virginia Bicentennial Center on Route 20 South at Interstate 64.

Skyline Drive and Blue Ridge Parkway. This scenic drive, one of the most beautiful in the nation, winds along the crest of the ancient Blue Ridge Mountains. The two-lane roadway twists and turns as it climbs from peak to peak and dips down into little valleys. Numerous overlooks along the way offer spectacular views. They also give you a chance to pull over and let the line of cars behind you pass. Traffic is often heavy in the summer and sometimes in the fall but at least you do

141

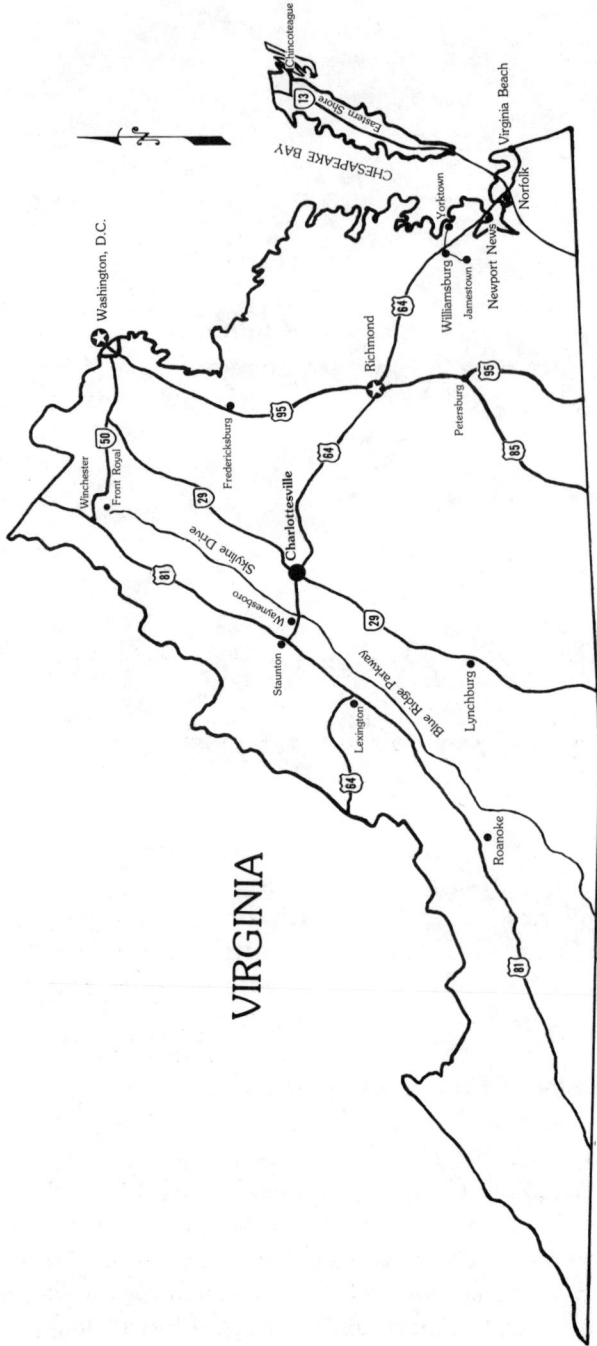

VIRGINIA

Washington, D.C.

Winchester
Front Royal
Fredericksburg
Skyline Drive
Charlottesville
Waynesboro
Staunton
Lexington
Blue Ridge Parkway
Lynchburg
Roanoke

Richmond
Petersburg

Williamsburg
Jamestown
Yorktown
Newport News
Norfolk
Virginia Beach

Chincoteague
Eastern Shore

CHESAPEAKE BAY

50
81
29
95
64
85
95
64
64
81
13

not have any monstrous trucks roaring and snorting behind you. To get to the drive, you can take either I-64 or Route 250 West. You can either go north on Skyline Drive to its end near Front Royal or south on the Blue Ridge Parkway deep into western North Carolina. There are attractive lodges and restaurants at Peaks of Otter, Big Meadows and Skyland, as well as camping facilities and hiking trails along the way. Reservations are needed during the season.

Shenandoah Valley. Maybe you would prefer to take the low road and look up at the mountains—on both sides—rather than look down into the valley. Interstate 81 traverses the length of the valley from Winchester to Roanoke. If you prefer a less-traveled—and more interesting highway—try the old valley turnpike, Route 11. The valley is full of history and beautiful farmland and orchards. Thomas Jefferson's land

holdings extended even into the valley at one time. He owned the Natural Bridge of Virginia, one of the nation's Natural Wonders, having purchased it in 1774 along with 157 acres of land for twenty shillings from King George.

Washington, D.C. Those traveling north may want to include a sightseeing trip to the nation's capitol, with its famous monuments, museums and the most politicians per square mile of any place in the United States, possibly in the world.

Richmond. Should you head east, Virginia's capital city will be on your route. You can take your pick of varied attractions—Capitol Square, with its beautiful Capitol Building, the main section designed by Jefferson; Monument Avenue, with its imposing statues; Civil War Battlefields; St. John's Church, where Patrick Henry is supposed to have uttered his oft-quoted "give me liberty or give me death"; and the nearby King's Dominion, a theme park featuring Lion Country Safari, the Happy Land of Hanna Barbera, Old Virginia, Candy Apple Grove and International Street.

Colonial Williamsburg. This meticulously restored Colonial village is well worth a visit. Spring and fall are the best times to avoid crowds. A few miles east of Williamsburg is Busch Gardens, where small "Old World" villages recreate the appearance of old towns in Europe.

Tidewater Virginia. There are many varied attractions in the Tidewater area. You can soak up sunshine and salt water at Virginia Beach and history and nostalgia at any number of places. Jamestown, where the first settlers landed. You can see a full scale replica of the old fort and the three ships that brought the settlers to this country. Yorktown, where the British surrendered in 1781. The National Park Service has restored a part of the town and the battlefields. Mariner's Museum at Newport News, with its world-famous collection of ship models, figureheads, paintings and numerous other things of ships and the sea. Hampton, Newport News, Norfolk—all offer sightseeing tours. And when it's time to

144

head for home, you may like to try the Eastern Shore route if you're going north. It's almost like going to sea when you head across the 17-mile Chesapeake Bay Bridge Tunnel that connects the mainland with the Eastern Shore. The scenery along the highway is a pleasant mixture of flat farmlands and small towns. If you have the time and like quaint villages and unspoiled nature, we recommend you stop off at Chincoteague and Assateague Islands. About five miles south of the Maryland line, turn right on Route 175. It's about ten miles—part of it across the marshes—to the old fishing village of Chincoteague, now a popular vacation spot. From Chincoteague you can drive across a bridge to Assateague, where the famous Chincoteague ponies roam wild and free. Assateague is a barrier island, thirty-three miles long, with wide beaches on the Atlantic Ocean. Wonderful for swimming and walking. The island is owned by the government and is a protected refuge for wildlife. Driving, biking and walking trails give you a chance to explore part of the island and see the birds and the wild ponies. A great place for nature lovers.

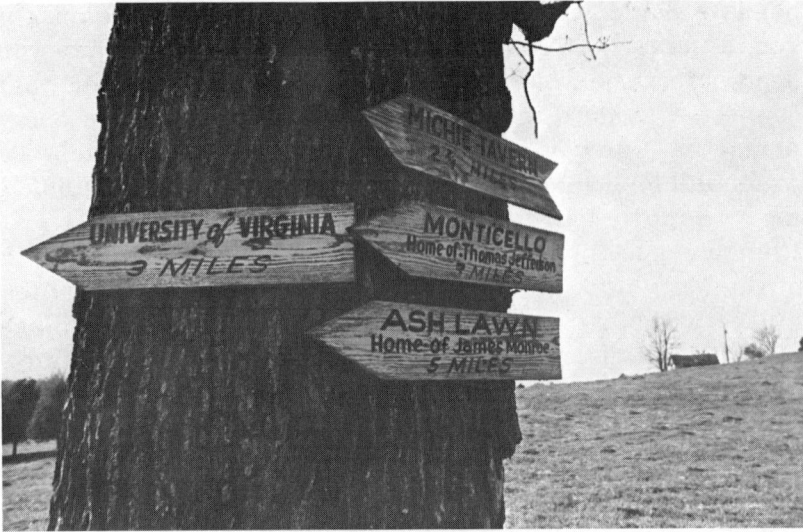

Locations, Hours and Fees
of Major Attractions

Ash Lawn
   March 1 - October 31   9 A.M.-6 P.M.
   November 1 - February 28   10 A.M.-5 P.M.
   Closed some major holidays.
   Adults $1.50. Children, 6-12, 75¢. Under 6, free.
   Rt. 53, two miles past Monticello.
   293-9539.

Castle Hill
   March 1 - November 30   10 A.M.-5 P.M.
   Closed December 1 - February 28.
   Adults $1.50. Children, 6-12, 75¢. Under 6, free.
   12 miles east of city. Rt. 250 to Rt. 22. Or I-64 (Shadwell Exit),
       then 250 to 22. East on 22 to Rt. 231, left on 231 two miles.
   293-7297.

146

George Rogers Clark Museum
April 1 - October 31   10 A.M.-6 P.M.
Closed November - March.
Adults $1.00. Children under 12, free.
Rt. 20 North, 1 mile north of 250 East.
295-1271.

Michie Tavern Museum
9 A.M.-5 P.M.
Closed Christmas and New Year's Day.
Adults $2.00.
Children under 12, $1.50.
Rt. 53 on way to Monticello.
977-1234.

Monticello
March 1 - October 31   8 A.M.-5 P.M.
November 1 - February 28   9 A.M.-4:30 P.M.
Closed Christmas.
Adults $2.00. Children 6-11, 50¢. Under 6, free.
Rt. 20 South to Rt. 53, left on 53.
295-9865

University of Virginia Tours
Monday - Friday   10 A.M., 11 A.M., 2 P.M., 3 P.M., 4 P.M.
Saturday - Sunday   11 A.M., 2 P.M., 3 P.M., 4 P.M.
For Prospective Students: Monday - Friday, 12:30 P.M.
                          Saturday, 10:30 A.M. and 11:30 A.M.
Abbreviated tour schedules during exams and holidays.
Schedules do change—check in advance.
No charge. Meet at Rotunda. (*n+icu*).
924-3239 or 924-7907.

Visitors and Information Centers

Charlottesville and Albemarle Chamber of Commerce
Monday - Friday   9 A.M.-5 P.M.
Closed Holidays.
100 Citizens Commonwealth Center.
295-3141.

University of Virginia Reception Center
9 A.M.-5 P.M.
University Hall. [Massie Rd. off Emmet St. (Rt. 29).]
924-7907.

Western Virginia Bicentennial Center
9 A.M.-5 P.M.
Closed Christmas and New Year's Day.
No charge.
Rt. 20 South at I-64.
977-1783.

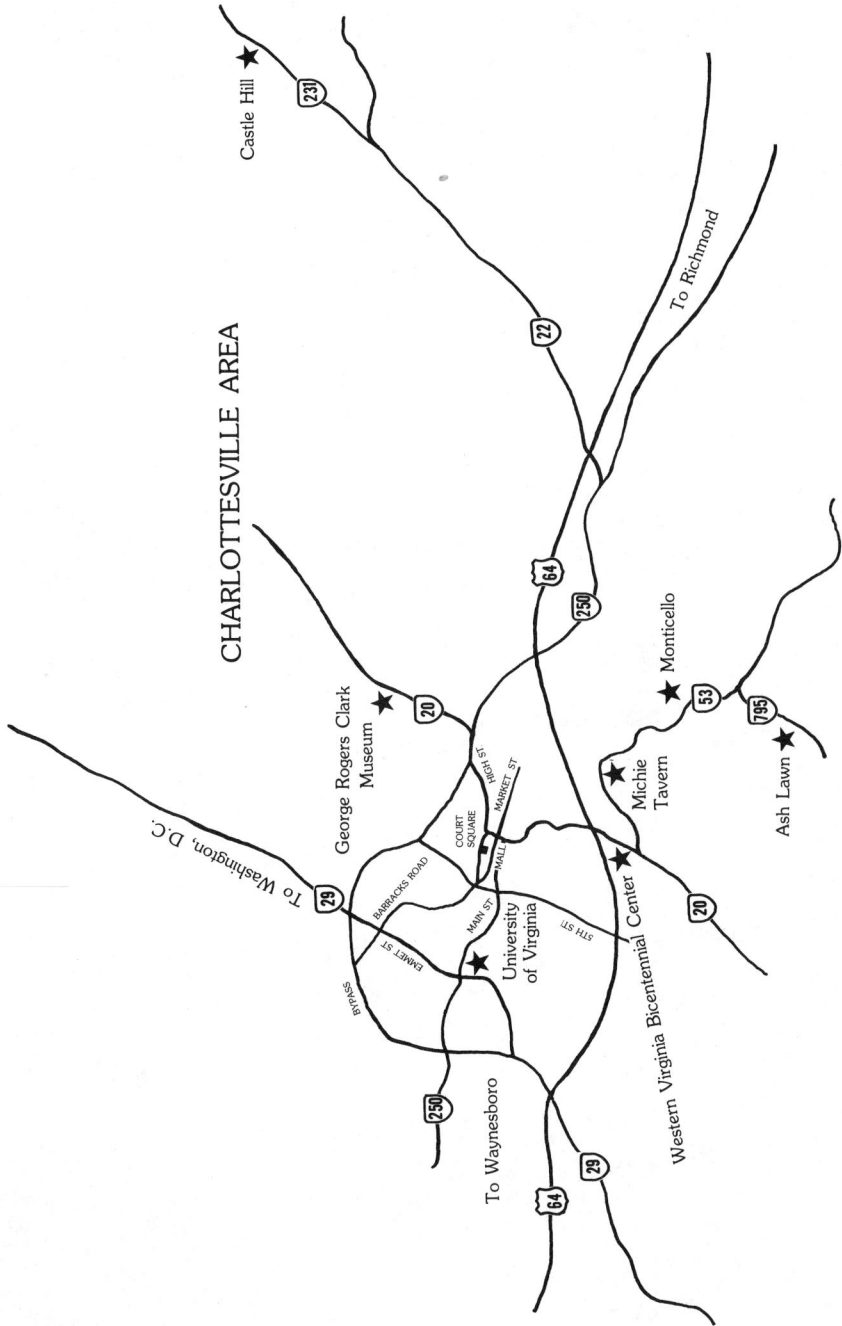

CHARLOTTESVILLE AREA

Castle Hill ★
231

To Richmond

22

64
250

Monticello ★
53
795

Michie Tavern ★
Ash Lawn ★

20
George Rogers Clark Museum ★

HIGH ST
MARKET ST
COURT SQUARE
MALL
MAIN ST
BARRACKS ROAD
5TH ST
University of Virginia ★
EMMET ST
BYPASS

To Washington, D.C.
29

Western Virginia Bicentennial Center ★
20

250
To Waynesboro

29
64

149

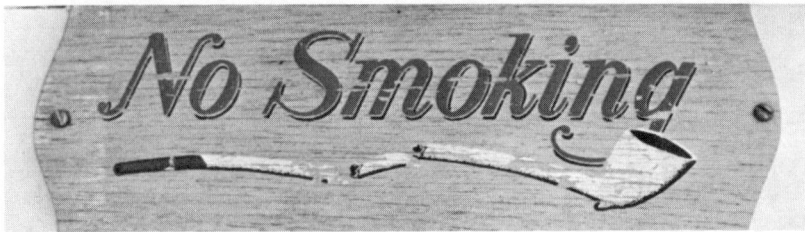

Emergency Numbers

FIRE 295-1125

POLICE 295-4151

Rescue Squad.................................... 295-1191

Sheriff... 296-2112

State Police.................................... 293-3223
    5 PM-8:30 AM 800-552-0962
    Sat., Sun. & Holidays

24-Hour Wrecker Service

AAA	104 Emmet	296-5631
Charlottesville Wrecker Service	1501 E. High (off 250 Bypass) Nights, Sun. & Holidays	293-8058 293-5252
JC Body Shop (AAA)	100 Meade Ave.	295-7082
Rivana Amoco Service	Rt. 29 N	973-5900
Marshall's Garage	Rt. 29 N Nights	973-4075 973-6680 973-4050 973-3165